The Ten Secrets of Heaven

By the same author

An Angel Healed Me

An Angel Spoke to Me

An Angel Changed My Life

An Angel Saved Me

How to See Your Angels

Celtic Angels

The Afterlife Is Real

Conversations With Heaven

How to Find Heaven

The Ten Secrets of Heaven

Mysteries of the afterlife revealed

THERESA CHEUNG

SIMON &
SCHUSTER

London · New York · Sydney · Toronto · New Delhi

A CBS COMPANY

First published in Great Britain by Simon & Schuster UK Ltd, 2016
A CBS company

1 3 5 7 9 10 8 6 4 2

Simon & Schuster UK Ltd
1st Floor
222 Gray's Inn Road
London WC1X 8HB

www.simonandschuster.co.uk

Simon & Schuster Australia,
Sydney

Simon & Schuster India,
New Delhi

A CIP catalogue record for this book is available from the British Library

Paperback ISBN: 978-1-4711-6246-6
eBook ISBN: 978-1-4711-5246-7

Typeset by Hewer Text UK Ltd, Edinburgh
Printed in the UK by CPI Group (UK) Ltd, Croydon, CR0 4YY

MIX
Paper from responsible sources
FSC® C020471

Simon & Schuster UK Ltd are committed to sourcing paper that is made from wood grown in sustainable forests and support the Forest Stewardship Council, the leading international forest certification organisation. Our books displaying the FSC logo are printed on FSC certified paper.

Contents

Acknowledgements

When I got news that my editor Kerri Sharp and her team at Simon & Schuster had decided to green-light this book, I couldn't have been happier. I danced for joy! I truly believe that each time a book about matters spiritual is published by a mainstream publisher it is a positive step forward. In today's often materialistic and unforgiving age we urgently need to consider the needs of our hearts and spirits and I sincerely hope this book will speak to and nourish the hearts and spirits of all those who read it.

As always my heartfelt thanks to all the sensitive, inspiring people who contributed their incredible stories to this book. I want you to know you are making a very real difference by sharing your words, your hearts and your spirits and bringing comfort, hope and light in the darkness. I would also like to thank anyone who has ever got in touch with me over the years via my angeltalk710@aol.com email and/or via my website www.theresacheung.com, or, more recently, through my Theresa Cheung Author Facebook page. You may not know it but you are a constant source of insight, inspiration and encouragement to me, as we all work together to spread the life-changing message that heaven is real. I would also like to express my gratitude and appreciation to Anita Moorjani and Dr Eben Alexander for their interviews and for bringing their light, wisdom and inspiration into the world.

My sincerest gratitude goes to Kim Nash, a remarkable lady with a passion for books (www.kimthebookworm.co.uk) and, as good fortune would have it, the afterlife. Kim's insight, hard work, brilliance and support on my social media sites is changing and inspiring the lives of my readers every day. Kim, you are an inspiration yourself. Thank you.

And finally, as always, a massive thank you to Ray, Robert and Ruthie for their patience, understanding and love, as I poured my heart, mind and spirit into writing this book.

First Words

What do I think happens when we die? I think we enter into another stage of existence or another state of consciousness that is so extraordinarily different from the reality we have here in the physical world that the language we have is not yet adequate to describe this other state of existence or consciousness. Based on what I have heard from thousands of people, we enter into a realm of joy, light, peace, and love in which we discover that the process of knowledge does not stop when we die. Instead, the process of learning and development goes on for eternity.

Raymond Moody

Earth has no sorrow that heaven cannot heal.

Thomas Moore

You must receive something of heaven into the soul, before the soul can be received into heaven.

John Thornton

Should You Read This Book?

There are more things in heaven and earth, Horatio,
Than are dreamt of in your philosophy.

Hamlet (1.5, 167–8)

Before you read this book please take a moment to reflect on whether it is actually the right book for you.

I always feel that reading a book that doesn't speak to your heart or mind in some way is like wearing shoes that don't fit properly. The shoes may look good when you first put them on, but then, when you actually start walking in them, you realise you've made a big mistake – they hurt! You wish you'd taken more time to make sure they were the right fit. In much the same way, I don't want you to read this book and regret spending your time or money on it. So, to discover if this is the right book for you, please read this next short paragraph carefully.

Whether you believe in heaven, would like to believe in it but aren't sure, or think it simply doesn't exist, there is one thing that must be accepted without question: we live in a mysterious world.

The universe is a puzzle, our consciousness is an enigma, and the meaning of our lives an unexplained mystery. Mysteries are things we live with every day and simply have to accept, regardless of how irrational and incomprehensible they are. So, if you are willing to accept that mysteries surround you and lie within you; if you are willing to open your mind to new and magical possibilities, the secrets of heaven are out there waiting for you to discover them.

If you can't relate in any way to these words, then this book isn't for you. It's probably best you try another title. If, however, you agree or empathise, or simply want to know more, this book has fallen into your path for a reason. You were meant to read it. I could not be happier. Time to begin . . .

About the Stories in This Book

Merely learning about the near-death experience has effects similar to those reported by NDEs.

Kenneth Ring

In the many years I've been writing about matters spiritual, I have gathered a huge body of anecdotal evidence for the existence of the afterlife – and the stories sent to me now number in the thousands. My correspondents never fail to touch my heart with their honesty. Some are already firm believers in the world of spirit – and their experience just confirms that belief – but many more were not believers, and what happened to them turned their lives upside down. They simply can't explain in a rational way what happened to them.

In the pages that follow, you will read a selection of some of the most memorable stories I have been sent over the years. Many of them focus on near-death experiences but others are simply stories from people who have seen or sensed a deep connection to heaven and/or departed loved ones on earth.

Every story offers powerful clues about the path to inner peace, joy and love, both in this life and the next. I have chosen stories that are clear to understand, so that anyone reading this book can see it with their mind's eye. In some instances, names and places have been changed to protect identity, and the stories edited for easier reading, but in most cases the stories here are lifted exactly from emails, letters, phone calls and interviews. I am deeply grateful to everyone who writes to me and I hope these letters and emails will continue to pour in, so I can share them with a wider audience. I firmly believe that the more people share their afterlife experiences, the more real and closer to earth heaven becomes. I also believe that the time could not be more perfect for heaven to reveal itself.

Details about how to contact me can be found on page vii.

Why is heaven talking now?

Global polls suggest that in recent years there has been a resurgence of belief in life after death, with up to ninety per cent of people trusting in the promise of heaven. There are a number of reasons for this. First and foremost must be the incredible advances in resuscitation techniques, bringing people back from the brink of oblivion with sensational near-death experiences (NDEs) to share. Fifty years ago, these people would not have returned to this life to tell their stories. Near-death experiences offer, in my opinion, perhaps the best proof we have for the existence of heaven. Medical studies confirming the survival of human consciousness after death, and the fact that quantum science does not deny the existence of an afterlife, are other crucial factors. The internet, of course, has played a huge part in connecting spiritually minded people together, regardless of their religion, and a number of bestselling books, spearheaded by Eben Alexander's million-selling *Proof of Heaven* and, more recently, Anita Moorjani's *Dying to be Me*, have also done much to strengthen belief and put heaven firmly centre stage.

With advances in modern medicine saving lives, and more and more people finding the confidence to share their NDE accounts online and in book form, it's now possible to paint a clearer picture of what lies beyond. It is also possible to gather vital clues from these stories as to what life in heaven may be like, and find out what is required from us on earth to enhance our spiritual growth and fulfilment.

In times past, ordinary people who had extraordinary experiences may have kept their stories to themselves, for fear of ridicule or contempt, but this is no longer the case, with talk of heaven and actually seeing heaven gaining mainstream acceptance. At a time of great change, conflict and upheaval in the world, I truly believe heaven is revealing the long-forgotten truths and revelations that once guided prophets, poets and mystics. These revelations are now being related through the stories of ordinary people who have travelled to the other side via near-death experiences and have had visions and dreams or other insights into the afterlife. In my humble opinion, the experiences of ordinary people are the ultimate revelation because they are a profound source of enlightenment, inspiration and guidance for us all.

I think we are at a unique moment in history, when the long-forgotten secrets of earth and of heaven are being revealed to us as never before. The problem is, the great majority of us are so busy with the fears, pressures and stresses of daily life that we have shut our eyes, minds and hearts to these important signs from the other side, even when they're clearly in front of us, waving at us for attention. It is up to each one of us to seize this unique moment in time. I hope reading this book, and the stories of people who have turned their lives around after heaven spoke to them, will play their part in opening your mind and heart to the very real possibility that miracles *can* happen and that heaven and life after death most definitely exists.

What lies ahead?

This book will uncover the secrets of eternal life that are hidden in true stories of afterlife encounters in NDEs and on earth. By uncovering these secrets – and getting as close as possible to the reality of the afterlife – you will discover what heaven is actually like and what your purpose in this life and the next is meant to be.

This life is topped and tailed by two miracles: birth and death. The search for life's meaning after we're born will be the subject of Part One – Secrets of Earth. In many ways it will be a 'how to' guide: how to be a spiritual being having a human experience and discovering your true identity and purpose. Part Two – Secrets of Heaven – will reveal the unseen realms that await each of us after death: the light, the warmth, the colour, the harmony, the joy, the beauty, the abundance, the wisdom, the love and the grace of heaven. From this we yet again learn that heaven is constantly revealing its secrets in our everyday lives in hidden but life-transforming ways, and once we know what these secrets are we can turn inwards, look upwards and unlock our divine potential.

Here you will discover the secrets of heaven . . .

> *For me personally, I'm showing more love to others now than before my NDE studies. My understanding of NDEs has made me a better doctor. I face life with more courage and confidence. I believe NDEs really do bring back a piece of the afterlife. When NDErs share their remarkable experiences, I believe a piece of the afterlife, in some mysterious way, becomes available to us all.*
>
> Jeffrey Long

Living in a Mysterious World –

A Personal Journey into Spirit

The most beautiful thing we can experience is the mysterious.

Einstein

My insatiable appetite for spiritual knowledge began with my mother. To say she defined who I am today would be an understatement. She devoted her life energy to the study of the paranormal, and in many ways I feel I am continuing her spiritual quest.

Like me, my mother never felt truly at home on earth. There was a part of her that always seemed to be far away. You can call it 'head in the clouds' or you can call it being deep and spiritual. Whatever you call it, she looked beyond the here and now, the everyday and the mundane, for a deeper meaning in everyone and everything. She made it crystal clear to my brother and I as we were growing up that she had absolutely no doubt there was more to this life than meets the eye. She repeatedly suggested that we were spiritual beings having a human experience and not the other way around. I accepted what she said as absolute truth. Her words became my inner guide and mantra and remain the case to this day.

I was naturally influenced by my mother's utter conviction that heaven exists and the afterlife is for real. I didn't have any confirming spiritual experiences, visions or actual proof of my own from which to draw conviction, but I never questioned what I had been taught to believe. I trusted my mother. I believed her completely. I believed in heaven completely. Being born into a family of travelling psychics and spiritualists, I witnessed countless spiritual meetings and demonstrations of mediumship during my childhood. I saw for myself how my mother, as well as my grandmother and great aunt, offered tremendous comfort and hope to those who had lost loved ones. I was in awe of these remarkable women and hoped that one day I too could have a similar beneficial effect on others.

So, from childhood till young adulthood, simply believing in the existence of heaven was enough to satisfy and fulfil me. I didn't crave anything more. I didn't need proof because I knew deep down that the most profound kind of faith is to believe without proof, but then, when I was in my mid-twenties, everything changed dramatically. It changed because life dealt me some tough and painful blows and I lost my sense of meaning, direction and purpose. Life didn't make sense to me any more. My spiritual beliefs didn't give me the resolve I hoped they would during challenging times. In fact, they gave me nothing.

Everything also changed because, when I was at my lowest ebb, my mother told me something that shattered and shocked me to the core. She told me her absolute belief in the world of spirit didn't 'just happen'. She had earned it, fought for it. She had absolute proof of heaven but had paid a terrible price for that proof.

When someone you love and depend on, because they appear so strong, calm and centred, tells you that at one point in their lives they tried to commit suicide, it can feel like a punch in the stomach. When that person is your mother, who has always made you feel safe and secure and taught you that life is a sacred gift, it can feel as if the entire world is crumbling around you. Was everything I believed in, everything I held to be true about this life and the next, a complete lie? I remember the moment exactly. I remember hearing the words, but the full meaning taking a very long time to fully sink in.

At the time I was working as a poorly paid supply teacher and had recently separated from my first serious boyfriend. The break-up had been sudden and painful. I thought he was my 'for ever boyfriend' but he turned out to be anything but. My heart was ripped in pieces and, because I had put my friends and career aspirations on hold to be there for him, as he would have tolerated nothing less than complete devotion from me, I couldn't seek solace from friends. I had no sense of clarity or motivation as far as my career or purpose in life was concerned. Money was desperately tight and, after moving out of my boyfriend's flat, all I could afford in London at the time was a room the size of a cupboard in a house shared with eight strangers, most of who didn't work. The house was right next to a railway station in Hackney and, every few moments, it felt like there was an earthquake as everything rattled. There were only two bathrooms in the house and one kitchen, and both were terminally filthy, as nobody cleaned up after themselves. My living situation was squalid and my heart and life felt empty, purposeless and squalid to match.

In short, I felt lost, extremely lost, so lost that I'm ashamed to admit a part of me longed for total darkness. I couldn't see a way forward. Life wasn't the magical adventure I had hoped it would be. It was more like a dead end. I didn't know how to exist without thoughts of my ex stopping me dead in my tracks. I missed him desperately, even though I knew he wasn't good for me and didn't care about me. Saddest of all, I also started to seriously doubt that this life had any spiritual meaning whatsoever as, despite my willingness to believe and my passionate hunger to see the other side, I had never personally been blessed with any direct contact from the world of spirit. I didn't have the 'sight' or the 'gift.' I felt like a failure on every level: personally, professionally, emotionally, intellectually and spiritually. I was in chaos.

My mother chose her moment wisely. She sat me down with a cup of tea and told me very calmly and matter of fact that taking my own life (I hadn't told her I was vaguely thinking about that possibility, as I'm good at putting on a brave face – she just sensed it) was a complete waste of time and effort and would not ease my pain in any way. She told me she knew this because she had almost died herself when she deliberately overdosed on sleeping pills. She had been in her mid-twenties at the time, just like me. Alone and penniless in London, she too had felt her life was utterly meaningless, and that there was little point to her existence.

I will try and cut a very long life story short here and tell you the circumstances that led up to my mother's suicide attempt as briefly and as sensitively as I can, in order to respect her memory.

A family in wartime

The early years of my mother's life had been blissfully happy. Born into an extravagantly wealthy and well-connected Dutch-Indonesian family, she was the adored, and some might say spoilt, youngest child of three, waited on hand and foot by housemaids. Her family owned the local theatre in Bandung, Java, as well as substantial areas of land in the area. However, when she was around nine or ten years old, she witnessed the full horror of Japanese-occupied Indonesia and the deep hatred towards the Dutch that the Japanese harboured at the time.

One evening, as the family was sitting down for supper, ten Japanese soldiers burst in on them with guns and knives. Just as she was eating her first course, the door to the dining room was smashed open. In shock, she dropped her spoon in the soup and later said she was more upset by the soup splashing on her new dress than by the aggressive intrusion. Her father had bought the dress for her the week before for being, in his words, such a 'happy, beautiful girl'.

The family was told to lie down on the floor. My mother's father, as well as her teenage brother and sister, were then immediately taken away by the soldiers and sent to separate concentration camps. There was no chance even to say goodbye or take any personal possessions. One minute my mother was an adored cosseted child in a happy and wealthy family, enjoying a candlelit supper, and the next her family and her life were ripped apart. Things were never to be the same again for any of them from that day on.

There was a flicker of mercy granted because she was a very young child and was spared the full horrors of the concentration camp. She was instead put on a ship bound for Holland to start a new life with my grandmother. Years later, she could still recall in vivid detail the overcrowding and misery on that grieving ship, but also admits that a part of her was excited because there was no school any more and it all felt like a big adventure. She was far too young at the time to understand the situation or fully comprehend the distress, torment and despair of everyone on board.

Once in Holland, she was teased and taunted by the locals for her mixed-race looks and exotic history. The teasing drove her indoors and, for the next four years, she barely set foot outside, living with her mother in a single room in a rundown house packed with refugees who, like herself, were from Indonesia. Then, when the war was over and she was fifteen years old, she had to endure the humiliation of going back to school with Dutch children who were several years younger. Children have a tendency to be very cruel whenever someone looks and speaks differently from them, and my mother was bullied relentlessly and treated like an outcast. Teachers did little to help, as their main concern was not my mother's feelings but classroom management. It was easier for them to isolate my mother from the group than discipline the class.

There is no doubt my mum's teenage years were distressing, cruel and lonely, but the same could be said for everyone who lived through the war. Lives were shattered and torn apart all over the world and there was the most unspeakable suffering and cruelty. Simply surviving the experience was a miracle. My mother did survive but the ordeal left deep and lasting scars that never completely healed. From then onwards she always suffered from hands that would shake uncontrollably. It used to make me laugh as a child. I would say, 'Mummy has wobbly hands,' and she would just smile at me and tell me this was because she was so happy and excited to be alive.

The war destroyed the hearts and lives of my mother's parents, my grandparents. When world peace was finally declared, they were no longer the same people. Joy and hope were drained from their souls and there seemed no way back to their pre-war happiness. They divorced and went their separate ways, and my mother stayed living with her mother in a single room. As for my grandfather, after spending close to six years in a concentration camp, he didn't even recognise his own daughter (my mother) when he saw her again. She rarely saw him after the war, and each time she did it was like meeting a stranger. She told me he looked at her and there was no flicker of recognition or interest. She said it was like they had never known each other at all.

As for her elder brother and sister, my uncle and aunt, they too were changed dramatically by their harrowing experience of captivity, and had very little interest in their younger sibling. They were too busy trying to rebuild and find meaning in their own lives. Effectively my mother's entire family was splintered, destroyed and a true casualty of the times.

My mother may have escaped the camps, but she didn't escape the sense of alienation, confusion, loss, crisis and deep pain that every member of her family experienced. At first she dreamed of becoming a violinist and joining an orchestra, as she was a naturally talented musician. With no money for lessons she taught herself to play the violin and auditioned for the Dutch Royal Conservatoire in The Hague. She must have been pretty good as, incredibly, she was offered a place. Sadly, though, she wasn't offered a scholarship, which was the only way she could afford the course, so she had to close the door on her musical dreams and accept any work she could to pay the rent and food bills.

At first she waitressed, but then taught herself to type and spent several years as an office assistant, although there wasn't much typing required and most of her working days were spent making tea and cleaning an office dominated by inconsiderate men, many of whom were sexist and racist. Her free time was devoted to taking care of her mother, who suffered from anxiety and depression, as well as constant bouts of poor health and joint pain after she had a fall.

Things came to a head for my mother when she was in her mid-twenties. She reached breaking point and could no longer cope. She knew she was slowly suffocating and, even though it meant leaving her mother, she had to get away to breathe some air of her own; to find out who she was. She wrote to her sister and brother and asked them to visit their mother regularly, as she needed to go away for a two-week, work-related trip. The trip was, of course, a fiction. What she didn't tell anyone was that she had packed her bags; she had set her heart on travelling to the United Kingdom and staying there.

Getting into the UK was no easy task back then, and at one point she actually jumped overboard so that she would be taken to hospital to avoid being sent back to Holland. With incredible generosity the UK allowed her to stay, as long as she found employment, but being penniless and with a heavy Dutch accent and Indonesian looks it was understandably difficult for her. Fortunately she was a natural linguist and she soon learned to speak English to a very high standard, so it didn't take her long to get work as a nanny.

After six months living in a woman's hostel close to Victoria Station, with no friends, little money and a job that involved catering to the whims of frequently spoilt children with indulgent parents, my mother felt she had seen enough of life. She felt just as trapped and alone in the UK as she had in Holland. Feeling there was no other option, she gathered as many sleeping pills as she could, visiting a number of different pharmacies so suspicion was not aroused, wrote a suicide note, went to bed with the note held tightly in her right hand, close to her heart, and hoped never to wake up again.

At the time, she was sharing a room with two other young women. She picked her evening to die carefully, thinking they would both be out until the next day, as they worked as maids in the same hotel and often did their night shifts together. And if they had both completed their shifts that night, then things would have worked out very differently and I wouldn't be here to write this book. On that particular evening, one of the women started vomiting and was sent home by the hotel. I'm sure she didn't think of her vomiting bug as heaven-sent but, from my point of view, that sudden illness was indeed a spark of the divine, proving that sometimes events that feel random or downright unpleasant to one person may be filled with meaning and hope for another. You see, without that woman being ill I would not have been born!

My mother was almost gone when she was discovered by her roommate and rushed to hospital to get her stomach pumped. During this procedure she had the most sensational experience. She isn't alive today to tell her story but I remember in vivid and accurate detail her description.

She told me this story only once, but every word remains engraved into my heart. As I type this it's like she is speaking to me. Of course, it isn't exactly word for word, but I assure you it is a faithful recreation of what she said. I'll relate her near-death experience in the first person because that is how I remember it.

Vital Signs

'Yes, my darling Theresa, I have seen the other side loud and clear. I've not told anyone about it until now, not even your father or brother. I didn't think I would ever tell you, but my heart is strongly urging me to tell you now because you need to hear what I have to say – even though I know you will think of my attempt on my own life as a betrayal. I'm so sorry, but there comes a point in every young person's life when their parents fall off a pedestal and they recognise that they're very human and fallible and don't have all the answers. It's part of growing up; it's part of you finding out who you are, separate from me. I know it's unsettling and frightening, but please listen to what I have to say. You will be glad you did.

First though, I know you're going to be curious about what happens when you die, so let's get that bit over with first. My journey to heaven lasted in earth time no more than three minutes – that's how long doctors told me they had lost me for – but I can tell you in spirit it felt like I was 'lost' for several days. Lost, however, is the wrong word, as when I 'died' I didn't feel lost at all. I felt I was exactly where I needed to be. Everything made perfect sense. That's what I remember most clearly about the whole experience – the complete lack of uncertainty. I knew who I was. I was pure spirit. I knew where I belonged. I was both in heaven and a part of heaven. It was the most comforting, fulfilling, perfect, calming, peaceful and beautiful feeling I have ever known. Very occasionally there have been blissful moments in my life since that have come close to that glowing feeling of belonging and vitality – giving birth to you and to your brother, for example – but I'll talk about other less-obvious moments in a while.

For now, let's get back to me, lifeless and fading away in hospital surrounded by doctors, with my legs hoisted up as my stomach was pumped – very undignified. One doctor even said that to another doctor. He said he felt sorry for me because I was young and had my whole life ahead of me, and what an undignified way to go. He also said I would probably be angry if they managed to bring me back.

How do I know all this? I know because I heard them saying it. I was hovering above myself, looking down at all the action. I felt a wave of pity then I was drawn back to my body and was literally face to face with myself, almost nose to nose, like I was pressing my face up against a mirror. I could hear doctors telling each other in urgent tones that I was coming back.

Then one of the doctors dropped something. It sounded heavy, and the sound distracted me. In an instant I darted away from my body again and found myself high up, close to the ceiling. What happens next is very curious. You would have thought I would be mesmerised, watching myself on the hospital bed, but I wasn't. What held my attention was a ladybird. There was all this frantic activity going on down below but it wasn't as interesting to me as the ladybird struggling and bouncing on the ceiling. I watched as its movements got slower and slower and then it fell to the floor. I don't know why but I wanted that ladybird to live and I focused all my thoughts on it. As I did, one of the nurses placed a glass over it, slid something flat underneath it and told the team she would take it outside, as it was still alive. I felt euphoric.

My euphoria carried me away somewhere at breakneck speed. I wasn't in the hospital any more. I was in a very dark and empty place but I wasn't scared. Quite the opposite: I felt very happy. The darkness felt like a warm blanket. I had this intense feeling of peace and calmness. In fact, the dark place – which didn't feel like a tunnel but more like I was in space – was quite refreshing, as I felt so light and porous. Above all, I felt I was letting go or being released in some way and there was this tremendous sense of freedom. I would have been content to stay in that dark place for ever, and at no point did I have any desire to return to my body, but gradually the darkness turned brighter and brighter.

Initially I felt agitated. I had felt comfortable and safe hiding, melting into the darkness, but now I felt exposed, as if everything about me could be seen, every atom of me open to inspection, like an X-ray. The openness wasn't painful or frightening in any way, just surprising and alarming. The only thing I can compare it to is being in a dark room and suddenly somebody switches on the light. It isn't unpleasant; it's just a mighty shock to the system and takes a while for the eyes to adjust. Well, it took a while for my spirit to adjust to heaven.

I'm not sure I did adjust completely because a part of me kept wanting to go back into the darkness. Having said that, another part of me experienced a sense of bliss and freedom, as my transparent spirit floated down into a garden, although the word garden feels inadequate and doesn't do justice to what I saw. In fact, all the words I'm using from now on fail because I'm trying to describe in human terms what is indescribable. I'm sorry I can't create a more vivid picture for you with my words, as words are not enough to explain what can only be experienced in spirit.

Gardens, streams and flowers are images that come to my mind but there was so much more. I also think that when you are in heaven you see things that you personally find beautiful and blissful. I saw strikingly magical scenes because that is how I imagine heaven to be, but I'm guessing other people would see different things that inspire or enchant them. I don't know. I can only tell you about my experience as best as I can. If I had artistic or poetic talent, it would be far easier for me to paint or write heaven. I think music captures it beautifully and if I could still play my violin I might be able to play something to evoke what I saw.

I can't say how long all this went on for because there was no awareness of time. The next fragment I remember is sitting on a bench beside someone I had never seen before. This unsettled me at first, as I would have liked to have seen my grandparents in spirit. I had absolutely no doubt I was dead and this was heaven. This woman was very pretty and in her thirties perhaps. There was a glow of pale, purple light around her. She was overjoyed to see me and I could feel her love towards me. I felt very comfortable and connected in her presence, but I'm not sure I felt love for her as such because she looked unfamiliar. She didn't have wings, so I didn't think she was an angel.

Then she told me who she was. She said that many years ago I had been one person ahead of her in a queue for cinema tickets to see *Sabrina* starring Audrey Hepburn. I bought my ticket but, when it came to her turn, the box office said the movie was sold out. She told me that when she walked away feeling disappointed, as she really wanted to see the film and didn't have another afternoon off for ages, I offered to give her my ticket. She jumped at the chance, bought the ticket from me and went to see the movie.

The woman went on to tell me that seeing the movie changed her life dramatically because she spilled her popcorn over a man, got talking to him, went out to dinner with him and, within six months, he became the love of her life. A year later they were married. She told me that she had been married only for five years before she died in a car accident, but those five years were truly magical. She had also given birth to twin boys. She said that if I hadn't offered to give her my ticket she might never have known what real love is. She might never have met her husband and her beautiful boys would not have been born. She told me that although he had married someone else now, this didn't make her sad; it made her happy because she wanted him to be happy. When he was happy she was happy too. She didn't want him to be alone. She also felt that her husband wanting to love again proved to her just how much he had loved her. His heart didn't shut down – his first marriage had been such a positive experience that he wanted to recapture it with someone else. Her husband marrying again felt like a celebration or tribute to her.

The reason she was waiting in my heaven to talk to me was because she wanted to know why I had done it, why I had handed over my ticket. I told her I noticed the disappointed look on her face and knew instinctively that seeing the film meant far more to her than it did to me. I just followed my heart. This answer seemed to satisfy her and the understanding made her purple glow even brighter. She nodded and smiled broadly. She reached out to hug me and, as she did, I felt this wave of happiness and euphoria.

I also realised in an instant the awesome power of random acts of kindness towards others – we may never know how our actions, even apparently insignificant and trivial ones, may impact others. And by extension we may also never know how things we think of as totally meaningless, like missing a train or getting lost on the way to work, may have a meaning because we are all connected and everything we do, however small or insignificant, influences others in some way.

I realise I'm digressing now, so let's get back to my vision of heaven. The woman then told me – although told is the wrong word, as she didn't speak; it was more like telepathy – that because I had been the reason she had experienced the transforming power of love on earth, she wanted to do something for me in return. She wanted to help me get back to earth. I protested at first and tried to explain how unhappy I was and that my life was going nowhere and I had nothing to live for, but she was having none of it. She told me that if I didn't go back I would simply take my unhappiness and despair with me in spirit. She explained that when we pass over our anxieties and cravings come with us. It's much easier to resolve feelings of despair in human form than in spirit form because despair and depression are human rather than spiritual emotions. In other words, I had unfinished business on earth and it wasn't my time yet.

At that moment everything went completely black and there was a sound like the cracking of a whip. I was back in my body. It was that sudden. One moment I was in paradise and the next I was regaining 'vital signs' in hospital. The medical team had brought me back to life. When I was able to sit up and talk, I told the doctor who led the team that saved me what I had heard and experienced. I told him somebody dropped something and how one of the nurses rescued the ladybird. He didn't tell me I was hallucinating. He just listened and nodded. He didn't comment except to tell me that what I had heard the doctors say when I was unconscious was accurate; someone did drop something and they had all noticed the ladybird and the nurse who took it outside.

Over the next few days I still felt bruised and battered. Surprisingly, I wasn't as elated as you might think by my trip to heaven. Perhaps, deep down, I have always known heaven exists, so the vision didn't surprise me dramatically. What lingered was the stern warning the woman had given me; that suicide was not the answer. My life had been spared because my soul needed to find peace and fulfilment on earth, but even though I had been to heaven and back I still wasn't sure how to find that inner peace. Dying wasn't the answer, but what was?

Fortunately I had to wait only a few days before heaven gave me the answer. I was about to take my first bath after a week of bed rest. The nurse had run the bath and it looked tempting but I couldn't help thinking there was little point. I didn't have the energy yet to be good to myself, to enjoy one of life's simple pleasures.

As I stood staring at the bubbles, a shaft of sunlight hit me square in the eyes. I squinted and tried to step away, but the shaft seemed to expand and cover me in a warm glow of sunshine. For a split second I felt the same way I had during my near-death experience, both when I was in the dark tunnel and then in the garden – peaceful, warm, comforted and free. It was magical – a sensation of overwhelming joy and calm. The feeling lasted only a split second but it was enough. It was like being wrapped in a fleece or a warm bath of complete bliss. It was similar to what I experienced when

> I crossed over to the other side. It was the reality of heaven on earth.
>
> I still feel it from time to time. I'm sure I experienced a moment of eternity both in this life and the next. My experience reassured me that I am a spiritual being and I have an existence outside of my body. Death doesn't fill me with fear. How could it? I have seen eternity. I am here now with you, living through a moment of time, but at any point I may glimpse eternity.

My mother then went on to tell me again, to drive the point home, that while she felt blessed and honoured to have been given absolute proof of heaven by her near-death experience – and she knew from that moment on that suicide is never the answer – her heart had still felt conflicted and uncertain. The real turning point came a few days later. What transformed her life, made her want to carry on living, wasn't her extraordinary journey to the other side but glimpsing eternity in something very ordinary – a ray of sunshine.

She concluded her story by telling me that light, warmth, mystery and magic could be found in the simplest of things, and if I wanted proof of heaven it was everywhere around me and inside me. I could find heaven in a grain of sand if my heart, mind and spirit were open enough. I didn't need the wake-up call of a near-death experience or full-blown angel or spirit sightings; they weren't necessary. She felt truly fortunate to be able to tell me about her experience. She hoped it would help me understand that hitting rock bottom or having a mind-blowing afterlife encounter were not essential ingredients to transforming my life and discovering the miracle of eternal life. I could find heaven in something as simple as a shaft of sunlight.

Then my mother asked me if I could remember a time when I was not alive. I felt really puzzled and told her of course not. She smiled and asked me to ponder this thought: perhaps I couldn't remember not being alive was because I had always been alive in spirit. She told me that she had, of course, witnessed my birth, but she knew without doubt that my birth wasn't my beginning, just as death wasn't going to be my end. I was eternal.

My head reeled after that astonishing conversation. We had spoken about matters spiritual many times but we'd never had a conversation as deep, powerful and mind-blowing as this. I didn't know whether to hug my mother or scream at her, so I simply put my head in my hands. When I looked up she was busy making another cup of tea. She knew that my understanding wouldn't come overnight. She knew I needed time and life experience to process all I had heard. She was right.

In the years ahead, when time and again I hit a low point and felt disillusioned, doubtful and alone, I would return to that pivotal conversation with my mother, and each time draw more understanding, strength and inspiration from it. I may not have witnessed the direct proof of heaven that she had, or have the psychic skills to actually see spirits, as she had, but I had something potentially more precious and helpful to share with the world: the secret knowledge that heaven reveals itself in the most ordinary but extraordinary ways.

Armed with this profound insight, I now had a clear choice. I could go back to my old ways and keep hoping for miracles, or I could start seeing miracles in everyone and everything, including myself. Or, to put it another way, I could choose fear and self-doubt or I could choose happiness. I could long for heaven to reveal itself to me externally or I could open my heart and start finding heaven for myself.

My mother's words also taught me another life-changing secret of heaven that impacted my life just as significantly, and continues to impact me every moment. Whether we know it or not we are all connected in highly complex ways, and while a single act – giving up your seat or ticket for someone else, or arriving five minutes late and so on – may appear inconsequential at the time, it is impossible to predict all the potential outcomes that may be triggered by this single act. We are all part of a system and, as my mother's experience showed, this system is not human but spiritual. To risk repeating myself, perhaps the greatest secret of heaven my mother revealed to me was that we are eternal spiritual beings in human form, and that in spirit we are all one.

A new world

There are only two ways to live your life.
One is as though nothing is a miracle.
The other is as though everything is a miracle.

Einstein

Although part of me sensed the compelling truth of my mother's words, I really wasn't mature enough to fully understand it at the time. It took me at least another twenty years for things to make sense. Even today I feel I still have more to learn from what my mother told me that day.

The path to understanding wasn't sudden; it slowly seeped into my being with gentle 'nudges' from the other side. These nudges took many forms, ranging from coincidences and dreams to signs and flashes of intuition that moved me forward in a positive way. But the nudges all had one thing in common: they moved me from a place of fear to a place of inner calm. They helped me see that many of the problems in my life came from fear, but fear isn't actually real. It is an illusion based on past experiences, which are somehow projected onto the present and future. For instance, at school I was constantly told by teachers I wasn't clever enough to succeed academically so, in the years ahead, even though I got into Cambridge University to read my degree, I projected this early assessment of my ability onto everything I did and was plagued by self-doubt. This self-doubt often sabotaged my chances of success.

The nudges from above also showed me that I was looking for happiness in all the wrong places. Arguably the most important lesson I learned from them is that heaven on earth has to be found inside yourself. If you can't find it there you won't find it anywhere. My mother found it within herself that day when she was recovering and about to take a warm bath. Even though she had had an astonishingly clear near-death experience, this glimpse of heaven wasn't the monumental breakthrough. Her desire to live life with joy in her heart only came after an inner transformation or 'peak experience'. She discovered heaven from the inside out, not the outside in.

Even though my mother told me as eloquently as she could that heaven has to be discovered from the inside before it can become real and manifest in your life, I still couldn't shake this unfortunate habit I had of looking for happiness in the wrong places. The habit had become ingrained because, for years, as I was growing up, I let my ego or fear replace feelings of love.

Fear and love cannot coexist in the human heart; it is a choice between the two, and fear claimed victory in my life too many times. I believed happiness was about relationships, having a great job, becoming a mother, looking great and so on. I wasn't completely wrong, as all these things contribute to a state of wellbeing and personal satisfaction, but even when I was in a relationship, had career success, a great job, or managed to squeeze into tiny jeans, there was always this lingering feeling of disillusionment and emptiness. None of what I thought would bring me happiness opened the door to heaven or feelings of inner peace. I thought that if I was loved, achieved things and looked the part, then my fear, insecurities and anxiety would vanish and I would be on the path to heaven. I could not have been more wrong. I had to learn the slow and painful way that happiness and a sense of self-worth can never be found on the outside. Looking inward for feelings of fulfilment is the only way to go.

Let me give an example that may resonate with some of you reading this. Often in my young adult life, I sought feelings of self-worth and happiness from relationships. There were probably deep-rooted reasons for this, in that my father was largely absent and uninterested when I was growing up, so where men were concerned I always felt inadequate or unworthy. My fears would manifest in co-dependent behaviour. I wrapped my world around the whims of my boyfriend and, unsurprisingly, when you lose yourself in someone like that, sooner or later they'll end up wanting to break free and you end up getting hurt.

It took the wise words of a stranger on a tube train to give me a shift in perspective. She told me that it wasn't worth crying over someone who wasn't going to cry over you. These words were the trigger for me starting to value myself a little more and recognising that a loving relationship involves give and take. If one person is doing all the giving and the other all the taking, this creates an unhealthy imbalance. For the first time in my life I asked myself why I was punishing myself caring for someone who clearly didn't feel the same way about me.

As soon as I started to question why I was treating myself badly, and why I wasn't loving myself enough, my motivations changed and wonderful things happened. It was like heaven opened a door and answers and illumination shone through. Around the time of this new awakening I had an amazing dream. I saw myself sitting alone on a see-saw, trying and failing to make it work. I stepped off and, as I did, another me appeared in front of my eyes. My dream twin smiled at me, ran to the other end of the see-saw, and beckoned for me to go back. I did and the see-saw worked. I woke up laughing. Could the message from heaven have been any clearer? The only person that could make me feel truly happy in this life and the next was me. *I* was the answer I was looking for. I needed to fall in love with my own spirit.

Falling in love with my inner spirit was a love I had never known before but, in the years that followed, it gradually filled me with deep inner peace. Since I was no longer searching for happiness in relationships or outside myself, I stopped being so needy. For the first time I felt whole and could say that I understood love. I knew it wasn't something anyone could give me or that I could 'earn'. I knew that it could be found in everyone and everything. I could find it when I walked in a park, enjoyed a cup of tea, read a great book, smiled at a stranger or went for a swim. Love was not something to be found but something I already had inside. Love was my birthright but, somewhere along the way, I had forgotten that and let fear take its place. With fear removed, love was my very existence. Love was infinite.

In much the same way I gradually learned, over time, to let go of the idea that I would know true happiness and fulfilment only when I could find proof of heaven or have a sensational paranormal experience. When I started collecting afterlife stories for my books I slowly but surely, without realising it, became addicted to the letters and emails people sent me. I tried to learn everything I could about visions of the afterlife and the power of mediums, wishing I could have that power myself. I attended courses, read hundreds of books, interviewed countless people and tried every psychic development technique you can imagine. Despite all this effort I still wasn't seeing angels. I still didn't have my own definitive proof like the people who wrote to me. Sure, I had the odd dream and stunning coincidence, but this wasn't enough for me. I wanted more. I wanted to see dead people like my mother and grandmother could. I was born into a family of spiritualists but I didn't have the gift. It made me feel like a failure.

One night, when I was in my early thirties, I was feeling particularly frustrated. I had been working for the previous few weeks on a series of articles about the psychic world. I had spoken to some remarkable people who told me incredible afterlife stories. As I listened to these people talking about heaven I could almost see them glow with happiness. They had an inner confidence about them I sorely wished I had. Despite my mother's incredible experience I still felt uncertain. I went to bed that evening wishing with all my heart to receive a sign in my dreams like the people I had spent the day talking to.

I did dream that night. In one dream I was climbing a mountain and in another I was visiting a museum, but neither dream seemed significant. I remember lying in bed the next morning staring at the ceiling and feeling a bit lost. Heaven clearly wasn't going to speak to me or give my heart any sustenance but then, as I closed my eyes, I heard a car pull up outside. As the car door opened I could hear the radio playing a song really loudly. It was one I'd heard many times before but this time it felt like a message from heaven. The song was *The Greatest Love Of All* by Whitney Houston. The reason it felt like a personal message was I suddenly remembered that in both dreams I had also heard that song playing. In my mountain dream I heard it as I climbed, and in my museum dream I heard it coming from loud speakers. I don't know why I had forgotten that crucial detail when I woke up. Perhaps because I was so fixated on dream images I didn't pay enough attention to dream sounds.

The lyrics of the song could not have been more powerful or more poignant: 'Learning to love yourself. It is the greatest love of all'. Yet again the universe was telling me I had an internal companion, an angel inside me, all the time. If I tuned into the love inside me – the love that had always been inside me since the day I was born but had along the way been pushed aside by fear because fear and love cannot co-exist – I would never be alone and would always feel the presence of heaven. United with the love within me meant I was connected to spirit. Just as my mother had told me, I didn't need to actually *see* spirit to have proof of heaven. Heaven was within me and all around me. Until I found the magic within me, I wouldn't see it around me. It was as simple as that.

All my life I had ached to have a connection with heaven but I had gone about it in the wrong way. Even though my mother had tried to point me in the right direction all those years ago, the fear inside me had still pushed me to look outside of myself – to relationships, to work, through afterlife visions – for validation. Now, however, I was at long last beginning to see that having faith in my spirit – my inner guide – was what I had been desperately longing for all my life.

My newfound connection to the love of spirit not only made me feel happier and more at peace than ever before, it also attracted a loving relationship, better work opportunities and wonderful moments of inspiration and revelation into my life. It may even have saved my life when I was at a busy junction one time and heard my inner voice speak to me. It was especially powerful because it sounded like the voice of my mother. The voice told me to take a right turn. Although I had intended to bear left before I heard that voice, I listened to it and turned right. If I had not listened to the voice I may not be here today because I would almost certainly have been involved in a traffic pile-up that claimed three innocent lives.

In the years that followed, heaven constantly found numerous ways to remind me of the life-saving importance of looking *within* rather than without for feelings of love and peace. It's a lesson I constantly need to be reminded of, and in that way I think I'm similar to many people. The famous song is right, as loving yourself is sometimes the hardest love of all.

To give an example, I had recently been let down by someone on a professional level and I was feeling confused and disappointed. The person I trusted turned out not to be a bad person, just not the person they said they were. I had a few weeks of frustration and broken promises and then, one afternoon, I heard the familiar ring of my angeltalk email. When I opened it I found to my astonishment that it was from one of my readers who had been inspired to write a piece of music after reading one of my books. I'm sometimes privileged to receive inspired paintings, poems or stories from my readers, but rarely the gift of original music. I listened to the track and it was the most beautiful piece of instrumental music I have ever heard. It was divine and made me cry with gratitude. I felt full of love and feelings of peace. A bit like Dorothy at the end of *The Wizard of Oz*, I realised that I already had what I had been searching for. The work I was currently doing and the inspiring emails I was receiving was all I needed.

I'd love you to share in the gift of this healing music. You can hear samples of it online on my website www.theresacheung.com as well as at www.cluainri.com.

The timing of this musical gift could not have been more perfect for my soul. If I could inspire just one person to write such beautiful music I was on the right path in life. I didn't need anything more than the readers I was already reaching. As if to underline the heaven-sent message, after listening to the track I glanced down and saw the most perfect white feather lying on the floor between my chair and my desk. How on earth did it get there? I didn't remember seeing it when I sat down. I knew instantly then, because there was a white feather involved, that heaven was trying to tell me something crucially important – something I thought I knew already but obviously needed to constantly be reminded of: I should not be looking for validation outside myself. I would never find validation there, even if my books were available all over the world it would not make a difference if there was emptiness within. If I felt let down, the reason wasn't because of external events, or the deceptive actions of others, it was because I wasn't supporting or loving myself enough.

The song and the feather were trying to tell me in a language I understood that the way we experience the world around us is a reflection of the world within us. If I felt unsupported or unappreciated or 'used' by other people, then life would reflect that back to me by letting people into my life who were going to disappoint or let me down or take advantage. The answer was to take responsibility and support and value myself and, in the months ahead, as I gradually made this simple shift from powerless victim to a person who believed in, valued and supported themselves and the work they do, I felt a burst of strength and self-belief again.

And to mirror that burst of self-belief and loving trust, and 'letting go' of the desire to force or make things happen with my books, wonderful writing opportunities came my way and my books reached new readerships, in Hungary, Poland, Bulgaria and Slovakia, to name but a few foreign countries interested in buying translation rights to my titles. My dream of seeing my message reach a more global audience was happening without me even trying. It was a tough learning curve, but a necessary one that I am grateful for. Now, every morning I repeat the same mantra to myself several times: 'If I feel unsupported or unloved, it is because I am not supporting or loving myself.'

All through my life the secrets of heaven have revealed themselves to me with gentle reminders like this, or through dreams, flashes of intuition, coincidences, the appearance of perfectly timed signs, like my song and the feather stories above, or with more dramatic interventions, like when I was saved by the voice of my mother in spirit at a busy junction. And, as I reach the second half of my life, I look back with the benefit of hindsight and see a clear and coherent pattern emerging. That is one of the joys of getting older: recognising the hand of heaven and realising everything happens for a reason, to teach you something or help you learn and grow, trust and love yourself and awaken as a spiritual being.

As I began to see a pattern in my life, I also began to recognise the familiar presence of these gentle secrets in the stories people sent me. The same profound life-changing truths hidden there were very similar to the ones I was experiencing, just with different people, places and situations involved. I could see that heaven was clearly sending the people writing to me the same message over and over, just in different ways. We were all being reminded of the constant presence of heaven within and around us. It was a revelation. It became abundantly clear to me that I had to use my understanding of the way heaven talks to us for a higher purpose than my own.

I knew that I was perfectly placed, in my role as a paranormal author, to share the life-changing power of these divine secrets and present them in an easy-to-read format for everyone to be inspired, guided, reassured and comforted by. The first place for me to start was, of course, my own life experiences but essentially everything I needed was right in front of my eyes in the stories sent to me on a daily basis by my readers. All the secrets of heaven and earth were there, waiting like hidden treasures to be discovered and shared with the world, to bring much-needed comfort, magic, hope, love and light.

PART ONE

SECRETS OF EARTH

And above all, watch with glittering eyes the whole world around you because the greatest secrets are always hidden in the most unlikely places. Those who don't believe in magic will never find it.

Roald Dahl

Everything you'll ever need to know is within you: the secrets of the universe are imprinted on the cells of your body.

Dan Millman

To dwell on the nature of the afterlife may divert us from paying attention to THIS life, where the lessons from the Light need to be practised . . . The true promise of the NDE is not so much what it suggests about an afterlife – as inspiring and comforting as those glimpses are – but what it says about how to live NOW . . . to learn from NDE-ers about how to live, or how to live better, with greater self-awareness, self-compassion, and concern for others. Live well, and death will take care of itself.

Kenneth Ring

The parable below, of the twins, is one I first came across about fifteen years ago. The author is unknown but you can find many versions and variations circulating on the internet.

Once Upon a Time

Once upon a time, twin boys were conceived in the same womb. Seconds, minutes, hours passed, as the two embryonic lives developed. The spark of life grew and each tiny brain began to take shape and form. With the development of their brains came feeling and, with feeling, perception – a perception of surroundings and of self. When they perceived the life of each other, they knew that life was good, and they laughed and rejoiced in their hearts.

One said to the other, 'We sure are lucky to have been conceived and to have this wonderful world.'

The other chimed in. 'Yes, blessed be our mother who gave us life and each other.'

Each of the twins continued to grow and take shape. They stretched their bodies and churned and turned in their little word. They explored it and found the life cord, which gave them life from their mother's blood. They were grateful for this new discovery and sang, 'How great is the love of our mother, that she shares all that she has with us!' And they were pleased and satisfied with their lot.

Weeks passed into months and, with the advent of each new month, they noticed a change in each other and in themselves.

'We are changing,' one said. 'What can it mean?'

'It means,' said the other, 'that we are drawing near to birth.'

An unsettling chill crept over them. They were afraid of birth, for they knew that it meant leaving their wonderful world behind.

Said the one, 'Were it up to me, I would live here for ever.'

'But we must be born,' said the other. 'It has happened to others who were here before.' Indeed, there was evidence inside the womb that the mother had carried life before theirs. 'Might not there be life after birth?'

'How can there be life after birth?' cried the one. 'Do we not shed our life cord and also the blood tissue when we are born? Have you ever talked with someone who was born? Has anyone ever re-entered the womb after birth to describe what birth is like? NO!'

As he spoke, he fell into despair, and in his despair he moaned, 'If the purpose of conception and our growth inside the womb is to end in birth, then truly our life is senseless.'

He clutched his precious life cord to his breast and said, 'And if this is so, and life is absurd, then there really can be no mother!'

'But there is a mother,' protested the other. 'Who else gave us nourishment? Who else created this world for us?'

'We get our nourishment from this cord – and our world has always been here!' said the one. 'And if there is a mother – where is she? Have you ever seen her? Does she ever talk to you? NO! We invented the idea of the mother because it satisfied a need in us. It made us feel secure and happy.'

Thus while the one raved and despaired, the other resigned himself to birth and placed his trust in the hands of his mother. Hours turned into days, and days into weeks. And soon it was time. They both knew their birth was at hand, and they both feared what they did not know. As the one was first to be conceived, so he was the first to be born, the other following.

They cried as they were born into the light. They coughed out fluid and gasped the dry air. And when they were sure they had been born, they opened their eyes – seeing life after birth for the very first time. They saw what they yet did not understand as they found themselves cradled lovingly in their mother's arms. They lay awe-struck before the beauty and truth they a few minutes before could only hope to know.

Why is it that, despite the awesome beauty and wonder of the miraculous world we live in, happiness and a sense of purpose and meaning seems to elude so many of us? It is all the more confusing for me as a spiritual writer why this is the case because I'm convinced from all the research I've done that happiness in this life is what heaven actually wants for each and every one of us. I think that while we are on earth we are supposed to live life joyously and to the full. Complications arise, however, when events conspire against us and we encounter problems, pain, injustice, cruelty and hardship. It is during such challenging times that we are truly tested and when we start questioning if there is a heaven or any justice in the world.

At these times heaven feels far away, but I hope to show you that heaven has never been closer – we just need to shift our perception and open our hearts and minds to the comfort, hope and inspiration that is all around us and within us.

Although I can't say I have all the answers, and I never will, because it's impossible to fully understand the unknowable in this life (just as a baby growing in a womb can't understand fully the real world outside), in the twenty or so years I have been writing about matters spiritual (and been in the privileged position of receiving thousands of letters from people all over the world about their spiritual experiences and insights) I have been able to identity common themes and laws. I am convinced these letters, and the amazing stories they relate, contain the secrets of a happy and deeply fulfilling life, however challenging, unfair and difficult things may sometimes appear to be.

Understanding these secrets can help you live your life in a deeper, more meaningful way and, by so doing, find your own unique path to heaven on earth.

1. AWAKENING

The first Secret of Earth is the importance of spiritual **awakening**.

There are, of course, those extremely rare individuals, whose souls seem to have been awakened simply by the miracle of their birth; who instinctively sense heaven within and around them, and who seem to spend their lives in a deeply contented and enlightened state, inspiring all who encounter them. For the great majority of us, however, this isn't the case. What tends to happen is that, as we grow up, the voices of fear and the destructive power of the ego systematically destroys the love and contentment inside us that is our birthright. This isn't necessarily our fault as, sometimes, for reasons we will never understand in this life, our souls choose deeply challenging circumstances or situations for us to be born into. Perhaps this is because our souls need us to experience something difficult, to help us learn and grow spiritually. I believe that everything is connected in some way to spiritual growth and is guiding us back to our true home, which is heaven.

When ego and fear rule our lives there is no room for spirit or for true happiness and peace, so heaven looks for ways to intervene in our lives, to help us 'wake up' and recognise the need to turn inward and re-evaluate what really matters. Sometimes this intervention has to be pretty dramatic or destructive to make us sit up, take notice and reassess. Sadly, the more we don't notice or try to ignore heaven calling our name, the more confused and unhappy we get.

Looking at the afterlife letters and emails and messages I get from my readers, and from my own personal experience, I think I've identified the most common signs that show the need for spiritual awakening.

The common signs of spiritual awakening

Dissatisfaction: Perhaps the most common sign – and often the first – is asking questions and feeling dissatisfied about the direction your life is heading. You may also start to doubt everything you once thought to be true or real. Sometimes these feelings of confusion can be very intense, and all your cherished beliefs and thoughts about yourself feel like they are crashing down around you.

During this period of confusion we are extremely vulnerable and may thrash about trying to find answers in philosophies, religion, spiritual movements or 'self-help' gurus, but the road to awakening is not one that can be found in an external group or set of beliefs. It can only be found within. It can only be found alone. It can only be found when you confront yourself, ask yourself who you really are, and do this with total honesty.

Sometimes looking within can cause personal pain and crises. Over the years I have received several wonderfully insightful emails from a woman called Judy. She too has been searching for change.

Inside Out

Theresa, everything you say in your books strikes a chord with me. Like you, I have sought heaven in countless different ways. I've joined churches, movements, cults, gone on retreats and study courses and thought I'd found the answer but have then come crashing down again. A year ago my marriage of eighteen years broke down and intolerable depression set in. I wanted to end it all but then, one night, as I had soaked my pillow with tears, I had the most incredible experience. I believe I saw an angel. I wasn't hallucinating. She was beautiful. She lifted her hands towards me and this ray of light shot into me, then she walked into me – it was like she dissolved inside me. Whether the angel was real or a product of my imagination I don't know, and I don't really care, because, from that moment on, I knew I would be OK. I knew that my despair was happening for a reason and that I was more than my physical body. I knew there was a shining angel inside me and she was looking after me.

As Judy's story shows, sometimes we have to reach our lowest point to awaken to our true selves and to the miraculous realisation that we are eternal spiritual beings.

Depression isn't the only catalyst for spiritual rebirth. You may feel that something isn't making sense about your life, or that you aren't moving forward in the way you would like. For example, you may lack a sense of meaning or purpose, or wonder if you have chosen the right career or relationship. All these life crises are signs that you urgently need to let go of limiting beliefs and open your mind to growth and change.

Confusion: Feeling confused, because you are experiencing unfamiliar feelings, is another indicator. Perhaps you thought you knew yourself well, but then you meet someone, or something happens, and you react completely out of character, surprising yourself and others. You may think you have found your soul mate or a new passion in life but, whatever the catalyst, your feelings are intense and you start questioning what you thought you knew about yourself.

Adventure: You may suddenly develop an adventurous streak and want to do wild or even dangerous things, like taking up an extreme sport or having an affair. As this typically happens as we head into our forties and fifties, it is often described as the midlife crisis. As long as you ensure that you don't hurt anyone who cares about you or depends on you, a midlife crisis is your spirit urging you to rethink your life and what truly matters to you.

Loss: You may see no way forward for yourself after the loss of a partner, job, friend, pet, your health, or anyone or anything that really mattered to you. Loss can be a terrible experience, but viewing it as a sign that you are ready to grow spiritually can ease things and help you grieve what you have lost before moving forward. Of course, the most excruciating loss is the death of a loved one. Your life is turned upside down, but this loss can often be a spiritual catalyst to changing your whole way of life. You may feel that your life has been destroyed by that grief, but if you call on the reserves of spiritual power inside yourself, you can learn to celebrate that person's life and enter into a new relationship with them in spirit. It's clear which path your loved one in heaven would most prefer you to take, and which path offers you the most healing and comfort. Confronting your own mortality – perhaps because you had a brush with death, are suffering from poor health, or because you suddenly realise life is too short – can also act as a trigger for spiritual awakening.

Search for meaning: You may find yourself drawn with deep intensity to matters spiritual and a desire to live your life with more meaning and purpose. You may also notice that your intuition is more accurate and you are sensing or seeing things more clearly or having vivid dreams; these all suggest that your psychic potential is developing. Your spirit wants you to listen to and connect with these psychic developments and make contact with the invisible world of spirit.

Learning from others: Another way for heaven to start awakening within you is through hearing the words or experiences of others and learning profound spiritual lessons from them. I recently interviewed some of the movers and shakers on today's spiritual world stage for my website and was struck by the number of remarkably similar events in their life stories – most significantly that there had often been great suffering or, indeed, in some instances, 'death', to get to the point where they are now. I'm going to digress a bit here but nowhere was this 'dying to see heaven' theme more striking than when I spoke to famous near-death experiencer, Anita Moorjani. If you read my interview with her over the page, you will see that she lived a life of anxiety and fear and endured terrible suffering and pain in the process of her physical and spiritual transformation from caterpillar to butterfly.

Anita Moorjani: Interview with the Catalyst

On 2 February 2006, Anita Moorjani had a near-death experience and came back to share what she discovered in her incredible *New York Times* bestselling book, *Dying to Be Me*. When I finished reading this book last year I had tears in my eyes. It is a book of courage and heart and wonderfully inspiring words for body, mind and soul. During the course of our interview, Anita told me that Ridley Scott's wife had a similar reaction when she read it, and passionately urged her husband to make a movie of it, which he is currently in the process of doing.

Anita admitted that she couldn't quite believe that her experience was going to be portrayed on screen, but she is grateful with all her heart that heaven has given her another powerful medium through which to promote her message. And that mixture of humility, humour and heartfelt sincerity is what makes talking to Anita and reading her book such a magical and moving experience. I just loved talking to this lady and I hope the love I felt shines through in the transcript of our interview.

Theresa: May I take you back to the 2nd of February 2006 and what happened to you in hospital?

Anita: Sure. I had been suffering from cancer for three years and experienced the hell and unbearable pain and loss of dignity that a cancer sufferer goes through, including rounds of unsuccessful treatments and chemo. On the morning I arrived in hospital, I wasn't able to move any more and doctors gave me hours to live. I had the most awe-inspiring near-death experience. I won't go into detail here, as you can read it in my book, but when I came back from visiting heaven my cancer just disappeared. It was nothing short of a miracle. Almost ten years on I am completely cancer free and every one of those days since has been a miracle. My life is a miracle.

Theresa: What did you learn from your NDE?

Anita: Just one thing, but the most important thing, and that is to be true to myself and to love myself. Before my NDE – and I'm sure what I'm going to say resonates with many women – I always thought it was selfish to meet my own needs before others, but now I know that if I do not love myself I can't give love to others because I can't give what I don't have. The more I love myself and am true to myself and have my needs met, the easier it is for me to be loving and generous to others.

Theresa: I agree with you, Anita, especially when you say women often feel it's selfish to put their needs first, but aren't there occasions when you have to consider the needs of another above your own, especially if you are a mother?

Anita: I see the point you're making, Theresa, and women do tend to put themselves last, but I'd like you to think about it this way: if you were told that everyone in your life, your mother, your family, your friends etc., did things for you out of obligation rather than heart, how would you feel? You wouldn't like it, would you? So my message is only do things from the heart. If there is no heart, ask or find someone else to do it for you.

Before my NDE I was a typical people pleaser. I always put other people first. I was afraid of being myself. I wasn't true to myself and always felt drained because I was doing everything not for myself but for others. I saw other people in need of help or less fortunate than me and thought I had no right to think about myself. Now I completely understand that it is not selfish to think about me or be here for myself and put my needs first. Indeed, as I think I said earlier, when I consider my own needs it makes me feel happier and healthier and more generous. I also know that in trying to be someone I wasn't, I was depriving others of getting to know the real me.

Theresa: Thank you for saying that, and I completely understand. I knew I was going to like you very much before we talked because I remember reading somewhere that your life rules include eating a little chocolate if it makes you happy?

Anita: Ha! Yes, of course. I'm all for anything that makes you feel happy as long as you are sensible and do it in moderation. I also recommend laughter and not taking life too seriously; enjoying your life and doing what brings you joy. Base your life choices on what makes you feel good and not on what you think you should do, or what others tell you that you should do. Fear of failing or disappointing others is also no way to live your life – make your life one of passion.

I often tell people to start the day with their favourite upbeat song – *Dancing Queen* does it for me – and sing along to it. I try to laugh at myself every day. I don't take myself too seriously because I know that the more I enjoy myself the closer I am to heaven. I laugh at myself a lot these days. I laugh at my flaws and no longer beat myself up if I make mistakes, which I do often. I laugh because I know to be human is to be perfectly imperfect and all I have to do is be myself and I can't get life wrong. I look in the mirror and tell myself I am a child of the universe and my only purpose is to be true to myself. I deprive the universe of who I truly am if I try to be someone else. It helps to start each day afresh and to forget about the troubles of yesterday. Think of each day as a blank canvas on which you can paint any picture you like. It really is your choice what you paint. You can paint with joy, love and laughter or with anger, worry, fear and regret. The choice is yours. Make it the best and most uplifting and positive choice for you.

Theresa: So could I sum up your message as simply as this: Be true to yourself and enjoy life?

Anita: Yes, you could. If you are true to yourself, you will enjoy your life and attract into your life what is truly yours. If you listen to your heart, and do things with your heart, you can't go wrong. The universe will oblige and help you. It really is that simple. The more you try to be someone you're not, the more you push away what you deserve. The reason we deny our own truth is fear – fear of not being good enough or pretty enough or clever enough or deserving enough. Just believe that you are enough and be yourself with joy and without fear and then you will attract what is truly yours.

Also, my NDE taught me a lot about forgiveness and relating to others. In my NDE state I knew the love for myself was unconditional and that I was one with everybody. I also realised that if people hurt me or are rude to me I do not need to forgive them. There is nothing to forgive because when people hurt others they do it out of their own pain. Or if we perceive hurt when there was no intention of hurting us then we are perceiving hurt out of our own pain. If, however, I love myself unconditionally and remember we are all part of the same whole, then it is so easy to love others unconditionally because they are all part of the same whole too, and forgiving others is the same as forgiving myself.

So, to sum up: if we live our lives from a place of total acceptance for self and unconditional love of self, it is easier to live in a place of unconditional love and acceptance of others.

Theresa: I know that the late philosopher Wayne Dyer had a huge influence on your life. I am deeply sorry for your loss.

Anita: Yes, it has been a very sad time and I miss him greatly. When I posted my NDE online I did it for cathartic reasons. I thought hardly anyone would read it. I had no idea it would go viral in such a short space of time and none other than Wayne Dyer would read it and help me get a book published about it. You would not even be interviewing me today if it was not for Wayne. I am beyond grateful to him for trusting that everyone should hear my message and giving me such an amazing opportunity to share it with the world. He has been my rock and my support. I miss him so very much but am grateful to the universe, as it could not have conspired to bring me to the attention of a kinder, more suitable and altogether wonderful person than Wayne. It took a massive amount of synchronicity for my online story to reach Wayne's hands and become a book in such a short period of time. I also feel deeply honoured that, since his passing, I have been asked to fill his mighty shoes in some of the talks he had been booked for in the months ahead.

Theresa: Apart from Mr Dyer, of course, who else do you admire or get inspiration from?

Anita: That's an easy question to answer. I am inspired by people who don't necessarily get recognition, money or praise for what they do but do it quietly anyway – the unsung heroes in this life. The parents who adopt foster children from challenging backgrounds or with special needs; the nurses who care for the terminally ill; the animal charity workers who rescue and care for abandoned animals. These are all people who bring heaven closer to earth but who most of us barely recognise. So I am inspired and humbled by the invisible angels in our society.

Theresa: And, apart from chocolate, what brings you the greatest happiness?

Anita: I was hoping you would ask that because my answer is so clear and simple: nothing makes me happier than to see others helped and empowered by my story. Every time someone tells me my experience has healed their heart I want to dance for joy. It makes all the pain and suffering I went through with my cancer so worth it. I would never wish that suffering on anyone else, so I hope I went through that pain so others would not need to.

I'd like to say that nothing would also give me greater joy than to see a world where people lived without fear. I understand that sometimes fear is essential because it warns and protects us, but the majority of our fears are irrational and eat away at us. I truly believe that fear and anxiety create illness because it wears down our immunity and it is also at the root of all the violence and cruelty that we see on the news. Our world today is very fear centred. Decisions are made based on fear rather than on a desire for joy and doing good things for ourselves and others. As a result, our emotions revolve around a centre of fear. Nothing – not even chocolate – would bring me greater happiness than to know that my experience, my story, my words, have been a catalyst for change and making people see themselves and this wonderful world differently. Our only responsibility is to be the change we want to see in the world.

Theresa: Can I take you back in time to before your NDE? What were you like? Were you the kind of person people wanted to talk to then?

Anita: Yes, I have always been the kind of person people seem to want to talk to, but back then I was ruled by fear and I was a people pleaser. I did things out of obligation and not from the heart. I was afraid to listen to my heart and did things to fit in. I felt I had to work very hard to be liked and would only be thought worthwhile if I did things that deserved it. I used to think being spiritual was all about hard work and I felt I needed to live up to other people's expectations. I now know with my heart, and from my NDE, that we are all spiritual and don't need to 'work' as such at all; we just learn to recognise and connect with it because we come from spirit and return to spirit.

And if I could go back in time to my teenage self – the one who hated herself so much and was bullied – I would tell myself to love myself just as I am. I would tell her she was perfect and did not need to change for anyone else. She has nothing to prove. She is loved unconditionally and her only purpose is to be herself.

I also used to be very particular about what I ate and would certainly avoid chocolate – it's been a bit of a theme in this interview, hasn't it? – because I feared gaining weight or being unhealthy. I was also afraid of getting cancer from certain foods or even sunshine etc. I now know that it is the feelings or emotions we have about what we eat that causes problems and not the food itself. If I eat food out of fear – even if that food is healthy – I'm just putting fear-based energy into my body, but if I eat food with joy and enjoy every bite I put love into my body. I hope this makes sense.

Theresa: It certainly does. Thank you. Do you feel chosen to do what you do now?

Anita: I believe I'm doing now what I'm meant to be doing. I know that because the universe helps me achieve my goals. The universe supports me. Things feel effortless and there is synchronicity all around to make my dreams a reality. I even had it recently when buying my apartment in California. A series of wonderful coincidences enabled me to get my dream apartment by the ocean. My soul needs to be close to the ocean. Everybody said what I wanted was impossible, as the area I had decided on had nothing for sale, but I just happened to bump into an acquaintance who knew of an ocean-view apartment that was going up for sale. I got there in time and bought the apartment of my dreams. When things are meant to be, there is that flow. I just surrender my ego's need to control and let the universe lead me. I trust my heart you see, Theresa. I know when I am living in a heart-centred way because all my decisions are present-based. With the brain, it is all about the future and there is fear and uncertainty. It is so much easier for the universe to help you when you listen to your heart and surrender to the love all around and within you.

Theresa: What about negative emotions? Do you have them? How do you deal with them?

Anita: Of course I have them. I am human. I don't deny they exist. I allow them to happen. I accept and learn and grow from them. Negative emotions are not wrong. They are part of being human. As long as you're alive you will have emotions, and thank goodness because emotions give us passion and power and the most dynamic and transformative and empowering emotion of all, is, of course, love.

I'm not one of those gurus who suggests hours of meditating or denying emotions to get closer to heaven. I think we are close to heaven every time we love and laugh, or get absorbed in something like walking or painting or singing or dancing, or our work, or the joys of family and so on. My kind of spirituality is a passionate one. I want everyone to live according to their heart.

I want everyone to turn away from fear and live fiercely. I especially want to empower women to do that, as so many women are afraid to follow their hearts, to trust their hearts.

Theresa: It was very moving to read about the deep love you have for your husband. I hope you don't mind this personal question but you have no children. Was that a choice or one life made for you?

Anita: I am truly blessed by the unconditional love of my husband. All I needed to do from the beginning of our marriage was love myself unconditionally too and, by doing that, I would love him unconditionally in return, but that didn't happen until after my NDE. Before my NDE, instead of enjoying his love I always felt I had to do things to make it up to him, to thank him for loving me. I didn't realise I just had to be his wife and that was enough.

Again, this is interesting. As women we often think we have to teach our husband, partners and children about the meaning of unconditional love, but my illness taught me that he was the one who was teaching me. My husband is my soul mate and he cared for me throughout my illness. He believes that was his purpose, to care for me, so he can now help me spread my message. I am forever grateful to him.

The chemo stopped the possibility of having children and that is difficult for me, as I believe I would have been a good and loving mother, but I believe things happen for a reason and now everyone who reads my story and my books, and one day sees my movie, feels like my child . . .

As I hang up I feel tears in my eyes, and pretty soon they are running down my cheeks. This woman has yet again touched my heart deeply, especially her closing words about everyone who reads or sees her story being like her child. I understand now why Ridley Scott's wife demanded her husband make a movie, and I understand why millions of people have been touched by her story and why, if anyone deserves to step into the shoes of the late Wayne Dyer, it is this remarkable, loving, joyful and humble lady. She truly is the catalyst she hopes to be for spiritual growth and making people see themselves and the world differently. Read her words and see her movie when it comes out and I guarantee you will feel better about yourself, more loving towards others, happier about your life, and more appreciative of this miraculous and beautiful world we live in.

Darkness before dawn

As I studied and talked to other great and good people who are today awakening the world spiritually, it became clear that a lot of these people, like Anita, have had a truly traumatic time before their awakening. This got me thinking. Perhaps they were experiencing and writing about their suffering, and how they found light at the end of the tunnel, so that the rest of us could learn from them and not have to experience the same kind of suffering. Although most of them would be far too humble to agree, I believe they suffered great hardship, uncertainty, pain and loss for our sakes.

Also interesting was that all of them said that before their dark and traumatic journey to spiritual awakening, they never felt they fitted into their own lives very well. There was a sense of feeling different, of being a square peg in a round hole, or not feeling that they had a sense of who they were or what their life meant.

In addition, they all agreed that their darkest suffering and turmoil or pain had been the catalyst for spiritual awakening. As if to underline this point, as I was writing this chapter I was invited to a tribute in London to the late, great Wayne Dyer, whose motivational books lit up the world and who, as mentioned in Anita's interview, discovered her story online. It was, as can be expected, an emotional evening, and footage of a talk he gave a few days before his death was shown. In that talk he talked about his moment of spiritual awakening.

Dyer said that for the first thirty or so years of his life he was obsessed with tracking down his absent father and that, although outward appearances suggested he had his life sorted, with a respected job as a university lecturer, inside he was deeply traumatised and unhappy. This manifested in addictive behaviour, relationship conflicts and a deep hatred for the father he never knew. When he eventually discovered his father's identity, it was too late to confront him because he had died. Still seething with pain and resentment, Dyer travelled to his grave with the intention of urinating on it! He cursed and swore for hours and afterwards sat in his car wondering why there was no sense of relief.

Then a miracle happened. He suddenly realised that the way forward for him was not to hate but to forgive, to understand that his father was operating from his own frame of reference, and did only what he could do. At that moment of forgiveness Dyer felt a painful burden lift from his shoulders. He drove to a nearby hotel room and locked himself away, writing, oblivious to the demands of his job and the outside world around him. The book that resulted was called *Your Erroneous Zones: Escape negative thinking and take control of your life*, and it was a self-help publishing sensation that inspired and healed the lives of millions and continues to do so to this day.

Spiritual awakening doesn't always have to be dramatic and sudden, as in the case of Dyer, or involve pain and suffering as was the case with Moorjani, or depression, as was the case for me. Sometimes the need for change can creep up on us unawares. In other words, you won't always know when you're ready or think you need to change. However, acknowledging that you are changing inside is crucial if you want to lead a deeper, more meaningful life.

If any of the above spoke to you, then this is a powerful indicator that you are ready to live your life in a deeper, more meaningful way. You are ready to leave ego, fear and limiting perceptions behind and awaken spiritually.

Rebirth

Awakening to, or becoming aware of, the possibility of a world of spirit existing beyond this life is the starting point, the root from which everything else grows, so I have lingered on it for longer than I originally intended, to demonstrate the importance of a strong foundation and/or catalyst on your spiritual journey.

To sum up, awakening spiritually really does feel like a rebirth. People who have had NDEs frequently say they feel completely different about their lives afterwards – but you don't have to almost die or suffer the depths of despair and confusion to be reborn spiritually. It can happen spontaneously without any effort or warning, or can gradually unfold from moments of bliss and calm. If, however, your new dawn is preceded by a period of darkness, crisis or loss of hope, the best way to cope is simply to accept what is happening, endure it and remind yourself that bliss can never be found externally but from deep within. Perhaps what you are experiencing is necessary for your soul to grow, and you may not understand the reasons until the next life.

Once you are able to 'let go' in this way, something miraculous will happen. You will wake up one morning with a peace in your heart and spirit that you have never known before. This doesn't mean you will have all the answers or will never again experience problems or suffering, but you will be able to approach the challenges that life throws at all of us with an inspired and joyful new perspective.

You will have had your first real glimpse of heaven on earth.

2. INSPIRATION

The second Secret of Earth is **inspiration**.

I recently watched a fascinating documentary about the racing car driver, Ayrton Senna. It was apparent that, from childhood, 'inspiration' was in his DNA. There were other superb, multiple-winning racing car drivers in his era but none touched hearts and souls like Senna. The outpouring of grief when he died was second to none, especially in his native Brazil, where he was and still is an icon.

But what was it about him that set him apart? He was divinely inspired, for sure, but why him and not anyone else? I think the reason was that he lived his life fearlessly and without any doubt that heaven was guiding and inspiring him. Every day of his life he faced the possibility of death but, because he believed in the other side without question, there was no fear, just calm acceptance and vitality in the present moment. He lived the power and magic of now.

I'm not saying we should all become high-speed risk-takers (because Senna died way too young), but perhaps we could look for the hand of heaven working in our lives and learn to live in the present moment with inspiration in our hearts, as Senna did. We could all commit ourselves one hundred per cent to something we believe in. We could treat every moment of our lives as a sacred gift from above. We could live our lives believing in the possibility of miracles rather than casually hoping for them. We can all be inspirations to ourselves and to others.

The miracle of birth

If you think about it, our lives begin with a miracle – the miracle of birth. For those of us who are religious or spiritual, a new spirit is born onto this earth from its home in heaven. For those of us who are not religious, birth is just as much a miracle in that a tiny, tiny fertilised cell can divide and divide and become a baby with a heart, eyes, mind and soul.

Conception science reveals that each baby born is a unique result of an astonishing merging of cells from the mother and father. From millions of sperm cells just one resilient soul converges with the egg. So this is how each one of us begins our life on earth, and wonderful lessons can be learned from this sensational process: the most obvious being that your very existence on earth is nothing short of awesome – a miracle. You are unique. Nobody else's DNA will match yours, ever. And you will also never again face such seemingly insurmountable obstacles for the right to breathe. The toughest part is already behind you. Please understand you have already beaten the odds just by being born. Seen in this light, virtually anything is possible if you are as persistent and courageous as you were from the very beginnings of your life, when your chances of surviving were just one in five million or more. In your day-to-day life, you will usually have way better odds than that.

So, when we consider that our very existence on this planet is a miracle, we have no excuse but to live each day courageously. We have no excuse not to be inspired by our own breath and by the beauty of the world we live in.

The story of your own miraculous conception is a wonderful source of inspiration, and hopefully it will remind you of something you instinctively knew as a child but may have forgotten along the line: how awe-inspiring the world is, and how precious every moment of life is. Each time our perspective shifts from one of stress and haste to one of gratitude and clarity, the more guided, inspired, loved and blessed you will feel.

Many NDE accounts describe feelings of blissful, intoxicating wonder and awe and inspiration on the other side. The people that come back to life, as John did, carry this heavenly feeling back with them, and it transforms their lives and the lives of all those who encounter them.

Colour Vision

Before my NDE I was one of those people who isn't unhappy as such, but isn't truly happy either. I was very functional, and saw the world around me in black and white terms. I used to dread art or creative writing lessons at school. The teacher would name a topic and everyone else would pick up their pens, but I could never think of anything to write or say or do. I settled into a career in accounting right after college, and my life became more and more routine; even when I got married and had four beautiful children routine was very important to me. All that changed when I turned fifty.

I'd had no history of heart problems, but I was driving to work one day and suddenly had these crippling pains in my chest and legs. Then I blanked out. Next thing I remember is waking up in hospital with absolutely no idea how I got there. Apparently I had swerved and hit a lamppost. Mercifully nobody apart from me got hurt, but my injuries were so bad I was in a coma-like state for days. My wife and children were told to prepare for the worst.

In the weeks ahead, as I slowly got better, my memory gradually returned. During that time, images kept flashing into my mind of unimaginable beauty, colour, richness, expansiveness. I'm using lots of words here because finding the right one doesn't do justice to what I saw. I remember an astonishingly bright light and I felt I was merging with it until I became the light. Then I found myself in a place or state where I felt such magic and joy. It was euphoric. Everything was turned upside down in that place but everything made sense. For instance, the grass laughed and the flowers sang and all was intensely alive.

I'm aware this sounds very peculiar, and a bit druggie, and that is why I haven't told anyone but you, but I want to tell you because I know what you will say – you will tell me I saw heaven. I don't know if I went to heaven or not, but what I do know is that I was touched by something. Ask my family. They'll tell you what a changed person I am. I have started drawing pictures of angels and have just had my first novel, called *Heart Beating*, accepted by a publisher – not a major one but you've got to start somewhere. The novel is all about something very mysterious – the workings of the human heart. I talk about my NDE and how it has changed me. I talk about love; not of other people but as a living force. I also talk about my emotional journey and how it took almost dying to discover my heart and the creativity hidden inside me. It feels like before my NDE I lived my life in black and white but now it is in glorious Technicolor.

Pointing upwards

From all the stories I have received over the years about NDEs or afterlife encounters, one theme comes through loud and clear: heaven inspires us to see astonishing miracles all around us every precious moment of our lives. Inspiration – like love, healing and beauty – is another word to describe heaven.

William Blake, the English poet who saw and heard angels all his life, famously saw the world in a grain of sand, so why not see spirit in a grain of sand, a raindrop, a sunset, a white feather, a passing cloud, the warmth of a hug, the magic of coincidences and answered prayers, or anything else that comforts and inspires you? Why not glimpse heaven in the soft breeze, in a bird's song, in the voices of people you love, in your heart and in your dreams?

Why not let heaven inspire you, work a miracle inside you and help you see the universe as it truly is: a place of unexpected wonder. Why not let heaven inspire you to see yourself as you really are: a miracle.

In short, anything on this earth that inspires feelings of wonder and awe, love and compassion and a sense of connection to the world of spirit, is pointing us in the direction of heaven and reminding us that there is more to this life than meets the eye. As these mini-stories show, inspiration can be found in the simplest of things and magic can be found in the most ordinary of places.

Ordinary but Extraordinary

Sometimes when I feel a gentle breeze on my face, I get the strong sense that my departed husband is standing close to me and kissing my cheek. You can call it imagination but I know he is there with me. I can't explain it. I get this warm glow and shivers down my spine. It doesn't happen every time the breeze blows, just sometimes, but when it does I feel like he is giving me a hug from the other side. I also sometimes feel him close to me when there is a beautiful sunset. We would often walk together and gaze in awe at the beauty of a setting sun. Now when I look at a sunset I believe he is still walking beside me. Janice

Heaven on earth – oh, that's simple! Every time my children laugh. That's when I feel I'm in heaven. Rachel

After my dog died I missed him so much. He really was my best friend. There is little support or understanding when a beloved pet dies, so I just carried on, but every now and again, and particularly after a long day at work, when he isn't there to greet me with his unconditional love, I get tearful. Anyway, about two weeks ago I came home and the tears were there again but this time I noticed one of his old chew toys – a panda – lying in the living room. I have absolutely no idea how it got there, as he had died four months previously and I had given all his food bowls and toys away to a friend who also owned a dog. I picked it up and it smelled so strongly of him it was like he was still with me. It gave me such comfort. I don't know why or how, but since then I've felt better and am even thinking of getting a new puppy. I know Panda (yes that was my dog's name ☺) would want me to do that. Paul

When you've had a hard day and are feeling stressed, it's remarkable how the smile of a stranger can lift your spirits. Happened to me the other day. I was in the supermarket and had loaded my shopping basket with too many items. I should have got a trolley but didn't have a spare pound, so I struggled with items falling out of the basket. Out of nowhere this lovely girl came up to me with the most beautiful smile and asked me if I would like her trolley. I said I didn't have a spare pound but I did have two 50ps. She happily accepted them and gave me the trolley, again flashing that beautiful smile. It really lifted my spirits. She reminded me a lot of my sister who had died ten years ago. She was always smiling and lifting people's spirits. It felt like she was there for a moment. Joanna

These stories show how nature, music, children, animals, and even something as simple as a smile, can bring a touch of heaven into our daily lives but, as each one of us is a unique miracle, each one of us will find inspiration – and a feeling that heaven is never far away and that miracles are possible – in our own unique way.

Remember, too, that if you look at yourself and the world around you as a source of magic, joy and heavenly inspiration, you are far more likely to find it – along with intense and deeply comforting feelings of closeness to those you love who are waiting for you on the other side.

3. COURAGE

The third Secret of Heaven on Earth is **courage**.

In my late teens, I got a job for a few days a week in an old people's home. I'll be honest here and say my first motivation for taking the job wasn't because I felt called to tend to the aged and infirm, but because my family urgently needed the extra cash. However, what began as a means to increase income ended up being a game-changer. I worked there for less than a year, but what I learned transformed my mind, my heart and my soul. I think everyone should have the privilege of spending time with those close to the end of their lives on earth, as it is a deeply humbling and empowering experience.

First death

It was the day after my eighteenth birthday when I saw my first dead body. I had no idea when I first came into the room with breakfast that the lady lying so peacefully, with a hint of a smile on her face, had actually passed away. I remember breezing into the room with the tray, then placing it down and drawing the curtains back to let the spring sunshine in. As there was no response to my wake-up visit, I gently touched her cheek. Her cheek felt warm and soft. I remember thinking how serene she looked and I'm sure at that moment I heard a deep sigh – one of those long, satisfying sighs you hear when people finally get to put their feet up at the end of a long day. I felt the breath of that sigh on my hand. I also saw her eyelids flicker. I was convinced she was going to wake up, so I talked about the day ahead and a chess competition that was planned in the home. When there was no response and her eyes didn't open, I stroked her face again. This time, in stark contrast to before, her face was icy cold. I knew then that something was wrong, so I rang the alarm button beside her bed.

Nurses were on the scene within moments and I was ushered out of the room by the senior nurse. I was in a state of shock, as I'd not expected this to happen – which was pretty naive considering I worked in an old people's home! For the next few hours I continued my duties in a bit of a daze. When it was time for my coffee break, I joined other members of staff and couldn't understand how they seemed to carry on as normal. Death was a way of life to them but it certainly wasn't for me.

A few days later it happened again. I came into the room in the morning, in just the same way, and immediately noticed an atmosphere of peace and calm that felt familiar. I knew the gentleman in the room had departed and I immediately raised the alarm. It took a minute or two for them to arrive, so I sat beside him and held his hand. It felt cold but my heart felt warm because the expression on his face was sublime. To be honest, he had been a bit of a complainer in his earthly life – never had a good word to say for anyone – but in death he looked content. Or should I say, the expression on his face was one of contentment because it was abundantly clear to me that this gentleman was no longer in his body; his body resembled a pile of clothes but his spirit – his essence – had gone.

That same week I learned that my first death, the lady, had died in her sleep and the coroner believed it had happened before midnight. I had woken her at 8.30 a.m. and I definitely felt and heard her sigh, so for me she was 'alive' then. To this day, I wonder if that was some kind of message sent from above for me – heaven telling me in a way I can't forget that death is never the end and there is life in death.

As you can imagine, working so closely with death in my late teens was a deeply profound experience and my job soon began to feel like a calling. I never knew from one shift to another if the person I was bringing food and drink or tidying up for or having a chat with would be there on my next visit. I learned an important lesson there, and it's one I have never forgotten, and that is to try as much as possible to make every conversation or interaction with other people as meaningful as possible. You truly do not know if that conversation or interaction will be your or their last. In the midst of life we truly are in death.

I'm aware I'm getting a bit morbid here, but spending time with people close to death does tend to sharpen the mind, pull your focus towards what really matters in this life, and makes you realise how much of what we think is important actually isn't. I am forever grateful that I learned this profound truth relatively early. Many people take decades to learn it. I am also profoundly grateful for perhaps the most significant lesson I learned from the dying, and that was to live a life of courage. Several of them had regrets, and wanted to talk to me about those regrets, and the constant theme that came through time and time again was wishing they'd lived their life with more courage.

But what is a life of courage?

A life of courage is one in which you are emotionally honest with yourself and others. It is also a life where you stop feeling guilty and simply give yourself permission to be happy. In other words, you are true to who you are and not what others think you should be. This sounds simple in theory but in practice it truly isn't. I think the best way to explain what I mean here is to tell you a story about a beautiful old lady called Jane, whom I befriended when working in that old people's home all those years ago.

About Jane

Jane was ninety-four years old when I met her. She was an extremely quiet woman with deep-blue eyes and hair so white and soft it looked like freshly fallen snow. There was something about her energy I liked immediately. I could tell she would have been a formidable woman in her prime. Within days I found myself lingering for longer than usual to chat with her and she began to tell me her life story. What struck me initially was how fascinating her life had been and how much she had done. She had travelled widely, enjoyed a career as a headmistress and set up charity-run schools in Africa. She also had six children and seven grandchildren. Her husband had passed away over forty years ago, but taking care of her children and her school career had kept her too busy to grieve.

Things didn't quite add up for me with Jane, however, as she had done so much in her life and had such a vast family but there were never any visitors. I asked her if her family lived abroad and she shook her head and said she hadn't had a proper visit from her children or grandchildren in seventeen years. They were like strangers to her. She said this in such a matter-of-fact way it made me want to cry. It was deeply sad.

I visited Jane as often as I could and enjoyed our chats. I toyed with the idea of getting in touch with her family, to ask them to visit, but it wasn't really my place. Two weeks before she died, Jane said something that went straight to my heart. She told me she could sometimes see me getting anxious and upset and that I worked very hard. She told me I deserved to lead a happy life without regrets. She said she had always felt guilty about being happy, always thought work was the most important thing, but what she didn't realise was that along the way she forgot to be happy – forgot how important it was to feel happy. She never had time for her children because she always thought she should be doing something else. She told me she regretted that bitterly and I should learn from that.

The next morning, when I went to see Jane she told me she had had a wonderful dream that she was with her departed husband and they were having a picnic and laughing. The following week Jane fell into a deep sleep. It took five days for her to pass, and during that time she only said one word over and over again – picnic. I think Jane was seeing the heaven that was awaiting her.

Years later, when I saw the film *About Schmidt*, starring Jack Nicholson, I was reminded of Jane. As the character Schmidt enters his retirement, the only person he is able to communicate with honestly is a little orphan boy in Africa to whom he sends money and letters but has never met.

If I could communicate with Jane on the other side and ask her what the secret of a successful, happy life was she would tell me what she told me in her final days – never be afraid to express your emotions honestly and with respect for the feelings of others.

And if I could ask the same question of Charles in spirit he would tell me to let myself be happy. He would tell me to let go of guilt and those pesky 'shoulds' and 'coulds' and just be happy. Here is his story:

Be happy

Charles was the very last patient I saw before I left the care home and went to university. He was an absolute delight. Had a filthy sense of humour but got away with just about anything, as he was so loveable. I wrote to him for two years after I left and when the replies stopped coming I knew he had passed but I also knew he had passed over smiling.

One particular interaction stands out. I brought Charles his afternoon tea and was feeling a little anxious, as my A-level results were due the following morning, and I knew the course of my future depended on them. Charles tried to make me laugh, as he always did, but he must have sensed my anxiety, so I explained. He then told me something quite remarkable. He told me that whether I got good grades or not it didn't matter because in heaven the only thing we're graded on is how many times we choose to laugh. He knew this to be true because when he was fifteen he had almost died after falling off a ladder while window cleaning. He had been larking about with a friend, throwing sponges and water from a great height; the ladder wobbled and he fell into darkness. He told me he went to heaven and met his great-grandfather there, who told him that heaven had loved the way he had passed over, laughing, but the gift he had of making people smile was so precious he needed to go back and use it.

Charles said he had never told anyone but me about what he had experienced, but it had informed his entire life. Of course, exams, career, earning money and all these things matter, but at the end of the day the only grade heaven is actually interested in is how much joy and love there is in my heart. Over the years I have, to my regret, often forgotten Charles's wise words, but time and time again memories of what he said have come back to remind, guide and reassure me.

True

I'll conclude this section on the theme of courage with a story about Alison – a lady I didn't meet at the old people's home, but whom I befriended during my university days. When I went to

Cambridge, I found out about a scheme where students from the university were encouraged to connect with elderly members of the community living in care homes, who, for some reason or other, were living isolated lives and needed companionship. I had grown and gained so much from my time as a care worker, that applying for this scheme came naturally and, for two of my undergraduate years, I would cycle every week to have tea and cake with Alison, a fiercely intelligent and beautiful lady who had been an international concert pianist, until arthritis prevented her from playing. She had never married – she told me music was her true love – and most of her family had died or moved abroad. This lady taught me so much about bringing heaven to earth that I don't know where to begin but I will try.

Alison's story

At seventy, Alison was one of the youngest residents in the care home. I'm not sure why she was there, as she seemed perfectly fit and of sound mind, but, for whatever reason, the care home was her place of residence. I didn't bond as strongly with her as the other residents, as I only knew her a few months before I left, but I did learn that she had battled against her parents' wishes to train as a lawyer and had studied music instead. They were so angry with her decision that they cut her out of their will in disappointment.

Life as a musician had been hard for Alison every note of the way. Earning a living and devoting herself to her music meant there had been no time for a relationship or family, but when I asked her if she had any regrets she said she didn't regret one single thing. Music had filled her life and her heart with joy and, when she couldn't play any more, her music pupils had given her joy too. She also told me that whenever she felt in need of comfort she just closed her eyes and remembered the magic of her performing days. She said that those days, for her, had never died, and that was why she believed in heaven – because her memories had never died and neither, she thought, would she.

Alison passed over on the penultimate day of my time at the care home. I had never attended any of the residents' funerals before but, for some reason, I felt called to attend hers, which surprised me, as I wasn't as close to her as some of the other residents. Her funeral was, as expected, not well attended. It was very simple and plain but that didn't matter. As I watched her coffin being lowered into the ground, I knew she had lived a beautiful life and had always felt the presence of heaven, and now heaven was welcoming her with open arms.

In the years that followed, my friendship with Alison continued to inform my life and my life choices. I went to Cambridge, and the expectation was to get a well-paid job but, instead, I followed my heart and taught health and fitness and started writing books about the same time. Helping other people feel good about themselves gave me such joy. Also, I stopped being embarrassed about my fascination for all things spiritual. With a degree in Theology you can imagine the criticism and disapproval I got and, to this day, still get when I tell people I write books about heaven and angels. There is always that awkward moment of embarrassment when people aren't sure what to say. I'm frequently not taken seriously, and my ideas are often attacked by intellectuals and scientists, but I stay strong and my readers help me stay strong. I believe in the existence of heaven and the life I want to lead is one in which I spread the word about the reality of the existence of heaven. I know it is my path because it gives me the greatest joy. It is me being true to myself.

Of course, it takes courage to be true to yourself and I have had many moments of weakness and fear along the way (and in all my books you can read about those moments and the ways I've found to emerge from the doubt and the doubters) but from all I have heard, read and seen, I believe heaven wants us to lead a life where we are true to ourselves and not backed into a corner by the expectations of others. It doesn't matter what the world thinks, or if others approve or disapprove, live the life you want to live and live it like that from this moment on because another potent lesson I learned from working with the dying is that this life is very, very short. The present, the now, is all we really have. Live it in the way your heart wants you to live it.

This exercise sounds daunting, but it really isn't.

Imagine you are close to a hundred years old and have but a few hours left to live. You are lying in your bed, perhaps surrounded by people you love or perhaps comforted by memories. Think about the life you are leading today. Would your dying self have any regrets about the life you're leading right now? Would your dying self urge you to make any changes?

If the answer is yes, then start gradually making those changes now, so that when your time comes you will have lived a life of courage – a life where you can say you have been true to yourself, so you can cross over to the other side feeling happy about your brief time on earth.

4. CONFIDENCE

The fourth Secret of Earth is **confidence**.

Being confident in yourself is the secret of a happy life, as long as you back up that confidence with a healthy dose of respect for yourself and others. Research study after research study shows that being confident empowers you and decreases feelings of uncertainty, fear and stress. But what these studies don't say is that confidence can also be a secret of a heavenly life.

Inside out

People who reveal a glimpse of heaven on earth tend to believe in themselves. The reason for their confidence is that, somewhere along the way, they have learned it is not selfish or wrong to love themselves, but, conversely, is absolutely crucial for their spiritual development. If you can't believe that heaven can exist within you then you stunt your spiritual growth, because, as this next story from Eva shows, the first place for heaven to reveal itself on earth is from the inside out.

Me Power

I've always been one of those people who used to say, 'It's only me,' whenever I came into a room or new situation. It was such a habit I didn't even think about until my ten-year-old son, Jake, bought it to my attention.

I was feeling tearful because it was the anniversary of my mum's death and I missed her very much. We had been very close and I used to call her every day before her death three years previously. I'd had a few dreams of her which gave me some comfort but I longed for a sign. Well, I think I got an amazing one. Here's what happened. I was taking Jake to a party at a friend's house, and when we arrived I knocked on the door and, before it opened, Jake grabbed my hand and told me he had had a dream of his Nana last night. He was playing chase with her but instead of saying 'You're it,' she kept saying to him. 'You're the.' He said it was really funny, like she didn't understand the game at all. I was so happy to hear that Jake was dreaming about my mum that I gave him a hug and started mulling the dream over in my mind because there had to be a meaning or a message from my mum in there somewhere.

The door opened, Jake's friend stood there and, before I knew it, I blurted out, 'The only me,' instead of my usual, 'It's only me.' It just happened. I just said it, and it felt so darn good, I said it again and again. The boys enjoyed my moment of madness greatly and started repeating really loudly, 'The only me, The only me, The only me.' We all laughed and then they rushed off to play, leaving me on the doorstep a totally different woman from the one who had knocked timidly on the door just a few minutes previously.

Sounds crazy but, from then onwards, I was no longer, 'Only me' but 'The only me.' It felt so good saying it. It was like a warm glow inside of me. I'm still not supremely confident, never will be as it's not my nature, but I believe on that day my mother in spirit sent me a sign through my Jake. She sent me a sign she knew only I would understand; a sign telling me that not only was she was watching over me but that I was unique and totally special and should stop undervaluing myself.

Looking inward

You need to believe that within you lies the power to create happiness and feel close to heaven. You need to trust in yourself and feel good about yourself. You need to *love* yourself. Sounds easy in theory but I know it's much harder in practice. I often have problems thinking of myself in a loving, magical way. I'm sure I'm not alone in this, and many of you may have also felt unworthy at various times in your life.

Trusting and believing in yourself is something we all struggle with. Your level of self-confidence or belief will likely ebb and flow throughout your life. It will always be a work in progress, and that's perfectly natural. Even the most confident, contented person still has bouts of low self-esteem, but there are things you can do and shifts in perspective that can help balance the scales again.

All too often our self-esteem is based on external factors: how we look, having a partner, climbing the career ladder, getting qualifications, having money and so on. But all this is so fragile and rather pointless because, as we have seen from NDE and afterlife accounts, in the world of spirit material things are completely meaningless. Also, the problem with self-esteem based on temporary externals is that you only feel good when things are going well. When difficult challenges are thrown in our path – which sooner or later they will be because, let's face it, we all age, lose jobs, fail in relationships, make mistakes and so on – you lose your confidence.

To prevent your self-esteem being controlled by external things, it helps to be grounded in self-acceptance. The concept of self-acceptance is based on the knowledge that we are all fallible human beings. We all have flaws and weaknesses and need to learn to accept ourselves, warts and all. Sometimes we say or do things we regret. Sometimes we get things wrong. Sometimes we are weak and needy. Sometimes we disappoint those we love and, in a world of billions of people there is always going to be someone cleverer, thinner, prettier, younger or more successful. That's life. So if you have convinced yourself that you just aren't good enough, you need to stop right there. Perfection in this life is not possible – indeed it is not even *desirable* because if you were perfect there would be no opportunity for spiritual growth and transformation.

Due to widespread misinterpretation of religious doctrines, many believe that only those who have lived a good, error-free life make it to heaven, but life isn't about getting it right all the time. Life is about getting it wrong some of the time and learning and growing from your mistakes. It is about confronting your demons and accepting that there's always room for improvement, because nobody can or should be perfect. Just imagine how dull and limiting the world would be if everyone was perfect! How could you grow spiritually if you didn't have inner conflicts to resolve?

So, to improve your self-confidence, focus on what truly matters rather than on material things; practise self-acceptance and stop beating yourself up if you get things wrong, because, try as you might, you are going to get things wrong from time to time. Doing the best you can really is enough sometimes. Remember too that building your self-confidence can take a lifetime (or more) to achieve, so don't feel despondent if you know you have a way to go.

I know from personal experience, and from countless stories I've received, that heaven certainly doesn't wait until self-confidence is high. In fact, it often breaks through when feelings of uncertainty, desperation or despair completely shatter self-belief. But I hope this fourth Secret of Earth shows you that you don't need to go through trauma, distress and shock and pain to find heaven. You can find it in quieter, happier, calmer ways, and in moments of warmth, serenity and inner confidence.

Falling in love

And last, but by no means least, the fast track way to achieving confidence is to love yourself more. Again it sounds all so simple in theory – and we all know on some level how vitally important self-love is for a happy life – but where to begin if you feel unlovable?

I know all about feeling unlovable, and if you've read some of my previous books you'll know I have often hated myself. However, you will also know that every time I moved from fear and self-loathing to love and self-respect, I opened a door to opportunity. In my books I often share with brutal honesty both the darkness and the dawn of my spiritual journey because I feel it's time the world stops thinking of anyone who writes, teaches or talks about heaven as some enlightened and highly evolved being. To think of a writer, teacher or guru as more perfect or special than yourself is to believe that person is living in a state of bliss and is no longer a part of this world. This kind of thinking just isolates readers or followers from their potential to find heaven on earth. Spiritual guides or teachers are just like everyone else – the only difference being they feel it's their calling to encourage others to search for meaning in their lives. But to see these people in any other way is damaging to your spirituality. I hope every book I have written goes some way to breaking down the barrier between my readers and myself. I think this will bring my readers closer to a recognition of their own divine potential.

I realise my approach here is unusual, as in certain circles the idea that a teacher is someone without flaws, or someone who had flaws once but has left them behind, still persists. Who wants to listen to or follow a guide who hasn't conquered their own demons? I have consistently challenged this ancient tradition and feel it is my calling to be as emotionally honest as possible, and to let my readers know about my doubts and my many flaws and insecurities. I get so many emotionally brave letters and emails from people telling me about their profound pain and despair, so how can I not be honest myself in response?

My aim when writing my books is, of course, to open people's minds to the idea that heaven is real, but I also have a secondary aim and that is to share my spiritual journey and how I have managed to pull myself out of dark places and times. There have been incredible highs but also many low points of self-loathing in my life but, each time, heaven found a way to pull me through, so I remain committed to showing other people how to find light after darkness.

What I hope my emotional honesty will teach you is that suffering and lack of self-confidence is a universal human experience. No matter how perfect someone's life looks or sounds, they still struggle with self-love from time to time. However, this can open up the possibility of tremendous spiritual growth, as it forces us to go within and to heal by finding ways to love ourselves.

It isn't self-centred, arrogant or selfish to fall in love with yourself. It energises us so that we have more love to give to others. We help the universe when we make love the centre of our world. You may have heard the phrase 'love makes the world go round' and, from all I have read and seen about the afterlife, I believe this to be the truth. Love is the bridge between this life and the next, between earth and heaven. Many people who have had a NDE say they don't judge themselves so harshly once they've had their experience; they love themselves because they have seen that love is the stuff of heaven and heaven lives within them.

The Language of Love

Crossing to the other side and coming back to tell my story has totally transformed my view of myself and others. When I 'died', I saw my life replayed back to me, and every moment of pain was caused by me not loving or valuing myself enough. It all became so obvious because I was in an ineffably beautiful place that only understood the language of love; anything not about love, of myself or others, didn't belong there. It's so hard to explain but, once you have seen heaven, felt the bliss and unconditional, all-consuming love, you can't get love out of your heart, head, body or soul. You know you are a part of heaven and, because heaven is love, *you* are love. If only everyone realised that in this life and the next, love of everything, including yourself – which can be the toughest love of all – is all that truly matters. To not love yourself is to not believe in heaven or the existence of heaven.

I had complete love and acceptance of myself in heaven and I wondered how on earth I could have forgotten that I was perfect and that I was pure love. Michael

For me, love is many things, but most of all it is a feeling of wonder and awe. When I talk about loving yourself, I mean finding a feeling of wonder for the absolutely unique miracle you are, even for aspects you may not think are very special. It breaks my heart when people write to me and tell me they will be happy when they find a partner, lose weight, gain a degree or are offered the job of their dreams. I want to tell these people to stop putting limitations on love and start loving themselves and being happy with themselves *right now* because as NDEs like those of Michael, show, when you do that you reveal heaven on earth.

You see, if you can't love yourself right now then you are not going to love yourself when you get what you think you want, because then you will find another excuse. Your only choice is to love yourself right now without expectations or conditions, because that is the unconditional love that will greet you in heaven. How do you do that? Simple: you just choose to love yourself right here, right now. You can make that choice immediately, and in time you will see it's the most selfless choice you could ever make, because when you love yourself you then have love to give to others – you can't give what you don't have yourself.

Your journey to self-love

This seven-step plan is a good starting point for your journey to self-love. As with any challenging journey, sometimes it will feel like two steps forward and three steps back, but the important thing is to keep going because you are on the right path. Keep looking ahead. Keep loving yourself and, as you do, you will lift up not only yourself but also those around you. You'll also bring heaven closer to earth in the process.

Seven steps to help find the light of self-love through dark times

Step One: Every single day, read this profound quote by Marianne Williamson:

'Never be afraid to shine or dream big for yourself again. Our deepest fear is not that we are inadequate. Our deepest fear is that we are powerful beyond measure. It is our light, not our darkness, that most frightens us. We ask ourselves, Who am I to be brilliant, gorgeous, talented, fabulous? Actually, who are you not to be? You are a child of God. Your playing small does not serve the world. There is nothing enlightened about shrinking so that other people won't feel insecure around you. We are all meant to shine, as children do. We were born to make manifest the glory of God that is within us. It's not just in some of us; it's in everyone. And as we let our own light shine, we unconsciously give other people permission to do the same. As we are liberated from our own fear, our presence automatically liberates others.'

Step Two: Inspire others

Look for the positive in others. Inspire them to be the best they can be. They say misery loves company but this could not be further than the truth. Just as you should not reduce or diminish yourself to encourage others to love you, don't reduce or diminish others either. Make others feel they can be the best. Once you start focusing on what is amazing about other people, it's amazing how these qualities start appearing in them and in you.

Step Three: Be your own best friend

Don't let yourself down any more. When you make a promise to eat healthier, exercise more, pamper yourself, study harder, keep that promise. Be your own best friend, the friend that never lets you down, but also a friend who loves you enough to tell you the honest truth when you need to hear it and give you a pat on the back when you deserve it.

Step Four: Celebrate

We are spiritual beings having a human experience but this is no reason not to celebrate the beauty of this human experience. Be grateful for the spectacular world we live in and the miracle of your human form. Marvel at the splendour of nature and at spectacular human achievements. Enjoy dressing to impress and looking your best as often as you can. Make your life an endless celebration of yourself and this beautiful world we live in.

Step Five: Set boundaries

If you encounter people in your life who are negative or try to limit you, then you need to respectfully set boundaries. Healthy boundaries are a natural consequence of self-love.

Step Six: Always be true to yourself

This is perhaps the most important step of all on the journey to self-love. If you are true to yourself, you are true to your heart. You are living a life of integrity, self-respect and love.

Step Seven: Smile and trust

On your path to the light of self-love there are going to be dark moments when you tell yourself you don't deserve love. Old habits die hard, but whenever that happens say the words 'smile and trust' out loud or in your thoughts over and over again. When you say these words you'll be reminded of past times when there was darkness, but the darkness passed. It is so much easier to love yourself and your life when you smile. So smile, even if you don't feel like it, because smiling will help you trust.

The fact that you're reading this book is a sign that you are more than ready to begin your journey to love. You are a spiritual seeker looking for the right direction. Start now. Take small steps. I'm honoured to be walking the same path with you, so we can all grow in self-love and together we can light the way ahead.

5. ATTRACTION

The fifth Secret of Earth is **attraction**.

The secret of attraction manifests itself on two levels. The first level is the relationships you attract into your life, and the next level is reflected in your thoughts. Let's begin with relationships.

Spiritual teachers

People who have had NDEs often report coming back to life filled with the desire to love everyone and everything. It seems that, once they have been exposed to the very highest level of unconditional love, they are changed for ever and this manifests in the way they show love to others. Their life has changed and the way they love others changes too – they no longer expect anything in return for the love they give. It is now unconditional. Here's what Sally has to say:

Connected

During my NDE I could see how my expectations about love had impacted all my relationships. I had a life review and learned that we are all interconnected to everyone and everything. My relationships on earth reflected who I was, as I attracted the energies of others that were similar to mine or extremely different, so I could fill a void. That's a 'wow revelation' – to know that the people in your life are part of you. It is human nature to want and to give love, and this creates our interconnection with each other.

You see, once you have felt this interconnection – as I had the privilege to do on the other side – you just have to have compassion for everyone and to care about them, whoever they are and whatever their age or culture. As your compassion for others grows, so does your understanding. Love becomes your state of being rather than something you need or take. You become part of the one great love and fly with it.

In heaven this oneness felt perfectly easy and natural but on earth it is not as straightforward. I struggle sometimes, but when that happens I remember my NDE and my life review and how I saw light rays connecting each of us and how my actions, thoughts and words affected others. I vividly saw an energy exchange going on, and intercommunication amid the interconnection. I think this is a transfer of energy and we have no idea it's going on, as it operates on a spiritual level. We exchange energy through every interaction and through thoughts and intentions.

If you think about it scientifically, we replace our skin, hair, nails, organs and tissues regularly, so it could be said each of us is a different person every ten or so years, when our cells have renewed themselves. We are also constantly breathing in the cells of others, and there is an ongoing physical interconnection or exchange between everyone you encounter.

Seen like this, we really are a part of everyone else, and what we think and how we live our lives affects those around us who are 'absorbing' us. In my life review it was unsettling to see how much confusion and pain was created when my thoughts and actions towards others were not in their best interests, and how living in a state of love and compassion made for positive, uplifting communication. It really isn't enough to pray or meditate or hope things turn out for the best; you have to live and love with an open heart.

Mirror, mirror

If we pay careful attention to the people in our lives, we will often see ourselves reflected back in a way that's truthful. By this, we can learn profound lessons about what is and is not heaven.

Relationships are impossible to avoid. They are the stuff of life. Whether it be parents and carers, partners, friends, colleagues, or the lady you meet every morning walking her dog, life is all about relationships. As the previous secret showed, the most important relationship you will ever have is with yourself, but each of us is also deeply involved, at every stage of our lives, with other people, who each play a part in shaping who we are.

The most formative years are those of our childhood, when we develop personalities that are influenced by our upbringing. But as life moves on, we evolve and learn to value connection, intimacy, and what it takes to maintain a friendship or relationship. We learn what falling in love means, the importance of give and take, and, as we adapt our personality and expectations to align ourselves with others, we are tested and challenged in myriad ways. Relationships can fill our hearts with joy and our eyes with tears. They force us to question and challenge ourselves. They can force us to grow. They can force us to give of ourselves. As NDE accounts make abundantly clear, our interconnected relationships act as spiritual teachers on this earth. From gathering afterlife stories over the years, I can now outline the most important spiritual lessons I believe relationships can teach us.

Back to school

First and foremost, I believe the people in your life reflect aspects of yourself back to you. If there is someone in your life who drives you mad or frustrates or limits you in some way, you need to think about how that person reflects an aspect of yourself that you may be struggling to deal with.

The flipside of this, of course, is relationships with people who love us unconditionally for the person we are. To be loved for no reason but because we are who we are can be deeply transformational. This is how we can learn through the eyes of another the power of self-love.

The second spiritual lesson relationships can teach us is the power of trust. When you love someone, you share a part of yourself with them in an intimate way. There are no guarantees they will honour your trust, but you give your love freely and in the process make yourself vulnerable. Of course, sometimes your trust will be betrayed, but that again teaches you an important lesson in that you need to understand why you put your trust in someone who did not feel the same way about you.

Closely tied to trust is belief – you've got to have belief in your relationships: belief that they are going to survive when things aren't going well. During those times, we learn how to cope with the bad as well as the good, and this helps us grow spiritually.

The third lesson other people teach us is respect. When we meet someone we like there is always that desire to merge into, control or lose ourselves in that person, because we often seek in others what we admire or lack in ourselves. If the relationship is to survive, we must learn to pull back as well as go forward. We must learn the importance of boundaries and respecting others.

The fourth lesson is a feeling of divine safety and protection. Being with people you love, and who love you in return, can give you a glimpse of heaven because when you are with them you feel safe and loved. You feel like coming home. Every near-death experience account I have read talks about this feeling of sacred belonging and warmth in heaven. So when you are with your loved ones you are in some respects experiencing heaven on earth. In addition, people who love us listen to, acknowledge and understand us. As we share ourselves and connect with them, they give us comfort and reassurance that we are not alone. The feeling is divine.

The fifth lesson is living joyously in the now. If you've ever had a chat with a friend and wondered where the time went – hours have flown by without you realising it – you are again glimpsing heaven on earth because you're living in the now, savouring the present moment without expectation, and having fun. The spiritual life is many things, but if I could find one way to define it, it would be living joyously in the present.

Lesson Number Six is the life-saving power of forgiveness. At some point or other in your life someone is going to hurt or reject you in some way. You have a choice. You can grow bitter and resentful and hold onto the pain of rejection or you can let the pain go and forgive them. You can think about the times when you may have hurt someone for reasons they couldn't understand. Such is the circle of relationships and of life. Hurt happens. We can learn from the experience. We can forgive as heaven forgives us and look ahead and move on.

The final lesson is perhaps the most potent of all and that is to learn to love others unconditionally. The people in your life will at some point let you down or not meet your expectations or needs. When that happens you can choose to reject or criticise them – and take a backward step spiritually – or you can love them unconditionally and accept them for who they are. This is especially the case if you have children, as children have a habit of challenging their parents on every level as they grow into adulthood. Children rarely turn out as their parents expect them to. Learning how to love someone unconditionally is the greatest spiritual teacher of them all. This means accepting and unconditionally loving your child, your parent, your lover, your friend – warts and issues and all. It is not easy, but if we learn how to do it, we learn how heaven loves us, and in the process we take a giant leap towards heaven.

Understanding the spiritual lessons other people can teach you is truly enlightening because every conversation, interaction and feeling you have about others can now be viewed in a sacred light, and as a way for you to develop and grow spiritually – a way for you to bring heaven closer to earth.

I think therefore I am

The secret of attraction is not expressed only in our relationships on earth, but also through our thoughts and feelings and what they attract into our lives. Many people who have died and gone to heaven come back with an understanding of how their thoughts have impacted and shaped their lives.

Veiled Spirit

Theresa, it was sensational. It was like I was in the centre of this endless vortex. Sounds mad, but I could see every thought and feeling and, the further forward I went down the tunnel, the more knowledge I received, and this knowledge came in thoughts and I soaked up every one. I felt the immense power of every thought, however trivial that it was. I saw the beauty of thoughts that empower and how that energy reflected back to earth. I also saw the ugliness of thoughts and the darkness they sent back down.

I was given so much knowledge in the tunnel and I absorbed it all. The floodgates of knowledge were opened. I remember thinking, 'I get it now. It all makes perfect sense.' I wondered how on earth I could have forgotten it but, of course, now I'm back on earth I've forgotten everything I absorbed except the euphoric feeling. I think in this life our human minds are too limited to understand, so a veil is drawn down, but I know from my experience that everything in this life is veiled spirit. Victor

All about energy

People often ask me to explain the law of attraction so it can be more easily understood, so this is a perfect opportunity to state it as clearly and as concisely as I can.

Quantum research has shown that everything in this universe and beyond is a form of electromagnetic energy. Matter is formed from this mass of energy through different arrangements, rates of vibration and density of the energy particles in the mass. Fire, for example, is particles of energy arranged in a certain way and within a certain distance. Change the arrangement and the density and you get smoke; arrange things differently again and you get ashes.

Everything is made up of energy – cells, molecules, atoms and particles (protons, neutrons etc.) and it is the arrangement, rate of density and vibration that makes the difference between a cat, a hat and you. You may be familiar with the term 'quantum field' – this simply refers to the 'stuff' everything (you, me, a tree) is made of and what we experience as form. There are other terms you can use, such as 'waves of probability' or, for me, 'unconditional love', but at the end of the day it refers to the basis of all creation. So how do your thoughts and feelings fit into all this?

Thought that is focused is a form of energy, just like everything else, and the same applies to feeling. If you have a thought and invest it with your energy you create an impression on the quantum field and, by so doing, start turning that thought into reality. If you keep that thought focused for long enough it can take physical form. So, according to the secret of attraction, whatever you focus your thoughts on most often is the thing you are most likely to attract into your life. This can work in both a positive and a negative way in that, if you want something enough, feel good about wanting it, and think about it enough, you are likely to get it, but if you don't want something to happen, and think a lot about how bad you will feel if it does, the chances of it happening also increases.

In short, whatever you think about most and have strong feelings about – be it good or bad – is most likely to enter into your life. You could compare it to a writer. He or she has an idea for a book. An outline or sample chapter is created and, in time, a publisher invests in the creation of a book. Things have gone from thought to manifestation in reality. So, think and feel good and the chances of good things appearing in your life increase. If you think and feel bad, expect to attract bad things.

There are three simple requirements needed to tune into the secret of attraction. First you need to ask. You need to think about what you want to be, do or have and how being, doing or having that thing will make you feel. Then you need to focus or concentrate. If your thoughts and feelings are focused, and you think about them for long enough, they will start to impress themselves at a quantum level and take form or shape. The final stage is often the hardest because we need to truly believe and expect our desires to manifest in our lives. If we start to doubt and lose faith because things aren't happening fast enough, or because we feel we don't deserve it, or fear our lives will collapse if we don't get it, we are creating blockages. Feeling good about what you want to manifest into your life is vital. Feeling bad about it just pushes it away.

Your feelings are always the judge and will usually tell you what you are going to attract into your life. You need to feel good, have faith and expect what you want to happen. Just trust and don't worry. You want the outcome but your entire wellbeing is not dependent on it. If you can get to that state of allowing, you are getting close to experiencing a state of bliss, or heaven on earth. You will notice that your life transforms in magical way. Not only will you be able to deal better with any challenges life throws your way, you will also be able to attract who and what you want into your life. You will be the master or mistress of creation and will be living a life of joy, meaning and fulfilment.

The law of attraction does have its complications, however, the most significant issue being the eternal 'why do bad things happen to innocent, loving people?' question. My response to this – I won't say *answer*, as in this life we can never fully comprehend everything there is – will be discussed in greater detail in Part Two: Secrets of Heaven. For now, try to get your head around the idea that the people in your life reflect aspects of yourself. They are here to teach you something. Your thoughts have far more power over what you attract into your life than you will ever, ever know.

If you want to explore this universal law further than word count allows me to do here, I urge you to read a magnificent and life-enhancing book called *The Secret* by Rhonda Byrne (Simon & Schuster).

6. INNOCENCE

The sixth Secret of Earth is **innocence**.

People who have had NDEs tend to return to earth with a twinkle in their eyes. They often tell me they laugh more than before and are more spontaneous and passionate about their lives. Whatever their age there is something refreshingly youthful, trusting and innocent about them. They are living proof that heaven is for the young at heart.

Young at heart

If you ever need a shot in the arm to remind you of the presence of heaven on earth, ask a child. Children have the sight, the innocence and the trust to see the miraculous that many of us lose as we age and when the cares and worries of the world start to wear us down. Children still possess that capacity for wonder, open-mindedness and innocence. This is not to be confused with being gullible or naive, but it does mean not shutting out whatever doesn't conform to reason or science.

I love hearing children talk about heaven. I love how they easily accept and don't question what they hear. They talk about heaven and seeing angels in such a matter-of-fact way, without a shred of doubt, and if I dare press them for details or clarification they often give me a look of surprise or pity that I need to ask them to make things clearer. To children it is simple and obvious that heaven is real, as this 'bliss on earth' story shows:

Making Sense

One Saturday I was driving Chloe to her swimming class. We were talking about birds. I'm an avid bird-watcher, and she asked me why I enjoyed it so much. I told her that birds were beautiful creatures with wings and watching them made me feel peaceful and happy.

'You mean like seeing angels,' she said.

I wasn't sure what to say but, before I could reply, she told me in a very matter-of-fact way that she could see angels. I'd never spoken to her about angels before and neither had my wife. We weren't into that kind of stuff. I asked her when she could see angels and she told me it was just before she went to sleep. Her angel would sit on the bed with her.

Later that evening I tucked her up in bed after reading a story. She was surrounded as usual by soft toys and I joked that there wouldn't be room for her angel to sit there. She started to move about in bed, squinting and muttering to herself. I wasn't sure what was going on but eventually, after a few moments, she told me that I was wrong and her angel was sitting on the bed.

Humouring her, I asked her what her angel looked like. 'Like anything I want her to,' she replied. I asked how she talked to her angel and she said, 'It was like pictures and thoughts and feelings.' Then she said that her angel was an old friend of my angel.

I asked if I could speak to her angel. She paused and said her angel wanted to know why I needed to talk to her. I replied that I was interested and wanted to learn. This seemed to be good enough because I was urged to ask away and ask away I did, with Chloe acting as a go-between me and her angel.

The first questions I asked were simple and fairly trivial, for example, if her angel had wings or if they lived in heaven. The answers I got were formulaic – angels can have wings and heaven is their home – but then Chloe went on to explain that heaven lives inside of everyone. This seemed a remarkably profound thing for a six year old to say. I went on to ask more insightful testing questions this time, such as what advice she had for me and Chloe, and each time I was astonished. It wasn't Chloe's imagination that surprised me, as children have fantastic and agile minds, but the quality and maturity of what she was saying. I would ask a question, she would pause and then, in simple, elegant words, reply with the kind of insight about life rarely seen in adults, let alone a six-year-old child.

I got the idea that Chloe's guardian angel did not so much solve problems or make life easier for her as provide a bigger picture of the issues involved; a clarity and life wisdom that helped to centre, calm and comfort her. Her angel did not hug her physically but reminded her that she was loved. When my daughter isn't speaking to her angel she is typically giggly and gorgeous daddy's girl, but that night, when she spoke for her angel, she was a profound and perfect angel interpreter.

Yes, it is possible that my daughter has wisdom and insight beyond her years, and there is no way I can verify the source of her inspiration in a scientific way, but what I can do is observe her. In the five years since we had that conversation – and many like it – I have seen her consciously, without previous schooling or training, tap into a well of insight, wisdom and love. And watching my child make sense of her life, by finding her own source of knowledge and comfort, has reminded me to rediscover my own. Mother of Chloe

I'm sure many parents and carers will have had similar experiences when their children show wisdom beyond their years. Whether you call it intuition or an inner angel, children of every culture, religion and race are born with a sophisticated sensory functioning that allows them to sense danger as well as love. Each child's ability to listen to and work with their inner angel is as natural to them as loving, learning and breathing.

There's a lot of talk these days about so-called indigo, crystal or star children. According to this theory, many children born since the 1970s are old souls who have highly developed spiritual skills. The idea is that these special children will remind us of the long-forgotten healing techniques of psychic awareness and immeasurable compassion. While there is much wisdom in the little ones of today, all my research on children and angels suggests that, in the eyes of an angel, all children, not just a select few, are naturally gifted and have much to teach us about living life in the now with energy, passion, trust, imagination, spontaneity and intuition – whether or not they claim to be able to see, hear or sense angels.

Children aren't perfect or faultless – far from it, as perfection is an unnatural state where no change or growth is possible – but whilst we try to teach children about life, more often than not it is children that can teach us what life is all about. And perhaps the greatest thing of all is that children can teach us to open our minds to the possibility that things exist even if we can't see them, and that there is always more magic and potential in this life than meets the eye.

Divine child

I've read countless stories like the one about little Chloe. Sure, you can dismiss it all as imagination or fantasy but the wonderful thing about children is their ability to suspend disbelief. It is this ability that makes children more receptive to spiritual experiences than adults. The term 'inner child' is a clichéd one but, like a number of clichés, it resonates with the truth. Carl Jung called it the 'divine child'. Emmet Fox called it the 'wonder child'. Charles Whitfield called it the 'child within'. Some psychotherapists call it the 'true self'. For me, it is simply being 'young at heart'. But what is the inner child?

The inner child is the child you once were, who desired to be nurtured, cared for and loved. This child still resides within you as an adult. It is the part of you that's innocent, sensitive, creative, emotional, spontaneous, playful, intuitive, passionate and enthusiastic, but also the part most in need of comfort, guidance, love and reassurance. As we leave childhood behind, many of us lose touch with our inner child and our ability to see magic in the world, but that magic remains with us all of our lives, even if it's buried under layers of responsibility. We are all children at heart, innocently searching for our meaning in life, and it is through our inner child that heaven reaches out to us on earth.

With love, trust and an open mind and heart, anyone, regardless of their age, can see, hear or sense the nearness of heaven in some special way. The thread linking all the afterlife stories I have been sent over the years is that the people who submitted them, whether they realise it or not, have the unique ability to see the world through the eyes of a child, whether or not they are young in years. It is this openness and emotional spontaneity that draws heaven closer to them. Seeing the world through a child's eyes doesn't mean being childlike in the sense of being naïve or ignorant of the ways of the world. It means having an open mind, accepting things in simplicity, and spontaneously expressing unquestioning wonder.

A child lives in a state of awe. Call it innocence, if you will. Untouched by worldly restraints and rules, children's hearts are free of mental slavery. They see the world through direct experience and live completely and precisely in the present moment. They don't see people as separate from themselves but as one giant family. In short, they see heaven on earth.

Heaven wants to speak to us all but most of the time we are just too busy and 'grown up' to see it. If, however, we open our minds and our hearts we can feel young again in spirit. Heaven is always waiting for us to pause in wonder and to ask the way with the trust and faith of a child. You don't have to be young in years to glimpse spirit but you do need to be young in heart and mind.

Extraordinary in the ordinary

If you want to experience heaven on earth reconnecting with your inner child, you need to cleanse your mind of fixed beliefs, allow your heart to do the thinking, and marvel at the magic and wonder of this beautiful world, as Louise did in her story:

Angels in the Cloud

One evening I was driving along a small country road. I decided to avoid the motorway, as it was a beautiful day and I wasn't in a rush. I was heading towards the sunset and there was a thunderstorm moving in from the north of the setting sun. The combination of the two natural phenomena created a stunningly beautiful sunset. I stopped my car and stepped outside to take a better view and only wished I'd brought my camera. My attention was instantly caught by a patch of drifting grey clouds that were illuminated by the rays of the fading sun. I swear to you that in those clouds I saw a host of angels. This was not a case of vivid imagination. Even though they were far above me I could see every detail of their faces. I

> could see their hair and their wings. They looked a lot like humans but with a glow about them. It was as if they were using the cloud vapours to reveal their beauty to me. It was so real and so true. It was not my imagination. I saw heaven.

Or to be inspired by the kindness of strangers and heavenly signs . . .

> Celia had recently lost her beloved husband Brian to brain cancer and was heartbroken. She had a nasty fall on her way home from the shops one day but was mercifully helped home by a kind man. After she had thanked the man and said goodbye she noticed a big and brilliant-white feather on her doorstep, and the kindness of the stranger and the feather (which made her think of heaven) helped her feel less alone and that she was being comforted and supported during a difficult and painful time in her life.

It isn't always easy to rediscover your child within, especially when times have been tough for you and people have let you down, or you switch on the news and witness unspeakable horrors. It is so much easier to become bitter and cynical in today's often conflicted world, but when you do that you just chase heaven and happiness further away. Keep your inner light shining and reconnect with the joy, passion and laughter of your inner child and heaven will begin to speak to you through your heart and through everyone and everything.

You will begin to see magic – the extraordinary in the ordinary. You will see and feel glimpses on earth of the heaven visited by people who have had NDEs or afterlife encounters.

7. KINDNESS

The seventh Secret of Earth is **kindness**.

Many people tell me they have become more compassionate as a result of their having an NDE. In heaven, compassion for all living beings and things was the only reality for them, and on earth their heart won't allow them to live in any other way.

No reason

There are always moments in our lives which burn into our memories and make a dramatic impact, and one of those happened to me when I was about eleven years old.

There was a girl in my class at school who was having a really tough time as her family had become homeless. She lived from one shelter to the next and missed a lot of school. Just before Christmas one year I was kept late at school for detention and this girl was staying behind too, probably to catch up on all her missed lessons. At the end of the session, as I packed my bags to leave, the history teacher came over to the girl with an envelope and handed it to her. She opened it and I could see there was cash inside. The teacher told the girl that every year all students' names were put into a hat and one was picked at random. This year, her name had come up.

At the time I remember feeling happy for the girl, and also a little disappointed I hadn't won the prize. I asked her what she was going to do with the money and she said she was going to buy her family a proper Christmas dinner. As I walked out of the room I caught the teacher's eye, and she put her finger to her mouth in order to request my silence. At that moment I instantly felt elated and understood what was going on here: the teacher had made up the whole story about randomly picking the girl's name out of a hat so that she and her family would not feel embarrassed or indebted to her in anyway.

I may have been only eleven but I recognised this as an act of real kindness. I was filled with a sense of joy and peace. As I left the classroom, life felt suddenly happier and I didn't have a care in the world. I remember skipping home and that feeling of joy and peace staying with me for days afterwards. In many ways it has never left me because I experience it every time I extend kindness without the thought of reward, or when I observe or experience the unexpected kindness of others. I couldn't think of a better place for Natalie's heart-warming story than here.

Angel at the Petrol Pump

I had the most incredible experience and I want to share it with you. It happened six months ago, a week before

Christmas. I was driving home and looking forward to a night in, as I'd done a lot of trips for work recently and it was good to have some 'me' time. Then I got stuck in an endless traffic jam and my car began to splutter and make strange noises. I started to get really worried when the driver behind me hooted and pointed to my exhaust. Dirt and smoke was coughing out.

Cursing my misfortune, I coasted to the nearest petrol station. I didn't want to block the traffic and I needed somewhere safe to see what was happening. As soon as I arrived, my car packed up completely, so I rolled into the forecourt and parked it out of harm's way. I tried the ignition several times but the car was dead.

I got out and took a look underneath. Everything looked perfectly fine so I got in again and tried the ignition but, once again, there was nothing – just a whirring sound. I was just about to call the RAC when I saw a young woman with two toddlers coming out of the gas station. It was a cold night and she caught my attention because she didn't have a coat on. She looked freezing. I watched her bend down to button up her children's coats and then, as she got up, she grabbed her back and yelled in pain. I've suffered from backache myself and I know it can be excruciating, so I really felt for her as she started to limp away with her children tugging at her. She managed only a few steps before having to rest against a petrol pump. With time on my hands I decided to get out of my car to check she was OK.

When I got to her I could see that she was much younger than I thought – barely out of her teens. She also had huge dark circles under her eyes. I could tell she was fighting back tears. I asked her if she was OK and all she said was, 'I can't let the kids see me cry.' She then went on to tell me that she was driving to stay at her sister's place. Life was really tough for her at that moment. She had left her partner because he drank too much and she was worried he would hurt her kids. She hadn't spoken to her sister for two years but she'd said she could stay with her while she got back on her feet.

As she spoke I watched her shivering and thought about my warm coat in the car and how the warmth would really be good for her back. The coat was a gift from my mum but I had several other coats and didn't really need it, so I rushed back to my car and gave it to her. At first she didn't want to accept it but I told her she was doing me a favour because I didn't want it any more. It was good to see her face look a little less pale when she put it on. I think the warmth of the coat also eased her back pain as she stood up straight. The children began tugging on her coat, asking for something to eat, but the girl shook her head. It became clear to me then that she didn't have enough money so, without hesitation, I took her inside the shop and bought fruit, crisps, sandwiches and other snacks. She gave the food to her children and they attacked it like wolves.

All the while she couldn't stop thanking me. I started to feel a little embarrassed, as I'm not normally the kind of person who does this sort of thing. I prefer to help others by writing a check [sic] or donating to a charity. Being this direct wasn't my style. However, something was urging me on and I knew deep down inside I was doing the right thing. I had a couple of painkillers in my bag so I gave them to her for her backache and helped her back to her car. Once she was inside I gave her my gloves and a £20 note and wished her well. She thanked me again and, as I started to walk away, she shouted after me, 'So are you like a Christmas angel or something? I've read stories about people like you.'

This time it was my turn to cry. I turned around and what I said next just tumbled out of my mouth. 'Christmas is a really busy time for angels, so sometimes regular people like me need to give them a helping hand.'

There have been times in my life when I've felt happy – like when I got my first pay cheque or when my boyfriend first asked me out, or when I managed to finally fit into a pair of size 10 jeans – but nothing can compare to the feeling I had that night as I watched that girl drive away smiling and waving at me. It was so incredible to be a part of someone else's miracle and to be able to touch someone's life in a practical way.

And, of course, you guessed it, when I got back to my car there was nothing wrong with it. I gave the ignition one last try and, to my surprise, it was working perfectly. I checked the exhaust and there was no dirt or dust spitting out. My car got me home with no problem. I took it into the garage for a service the next day and the mechanic didn't find anything wrong either, which makes me think that I was meant to stop at that petrol station so that I could give that girl – I don't even know her name – the warmth, support and hope she so urgently needed.

This story reminds us that everything we do and say has the potential to touch others in a heavenly way. Whenever you feel love or compassion for someone you are being an angel from heaven. A single happy smile can brighten someone else's day; a kind and gentle word can make a great difference by helping someone find peace in their life, and a little bit of thoughtfulness or a tiny act of kindness can create a ray of sunshine in the lives of others. This next mini-story, I don't know the exact source, says it perfectly.

> On the street I saw a little boy cold and shivering in a thin pair of shorts and a threadbare shirt. I became angry and asked the angels, 'Why did you permit this? Why don't you do something about it?' My guardian angel replied, 'I certainly did do something about it ... I brought you here.'

Being kind, witnessing the kindness of others or reading about it, can offer us a glimpse of heaven on earth by filling us with feelings of awe, wonder and intense gratitude for being alive. As you'll see from the mini-stories below, even the simplest altruistic acts can radiate bliss.

> I bought a homeless man a cup of tea and a muffin this winter. He was standing in the bus shelter as it was so cold. It felt so good to do something nice.' Luke

> 'I love cats, got six of them. One went missing and I was distraught but I got a phone call from a gentleman who had found her. I went round and my cat was sitting on the lap of

this man's daughter, purring. The man told me that his wife had died a month ago and my cat had made his daughter smile again. I let them keep my cat. I knew it was the right thing to do because I left their house feeling happy. Wanda

Sounds funny, but whenever someone offers me their car park ticket with free time left on it, it feels so right. Katy

The lovely feeling of surprise I got when my wallet was returned to me anonymously with everything – cash, cards, photo intact. Paul

I was feeling low as my exam results meant I couldn't go to the university I wanted. I had to get some shopping and, as I was going into the shop, an elderly lady arrived at the same time. I stepped back and held open the door for her. As I did so she gave my arm a gentle tug and flashed such a comforting smile. I felt like an angel was blessing me. A smile and a gentle touch really can change things. I felt so much better about myself and my future after that and realised that if my first-choice university wasn't the way ahead then it was for a reason. Turns out I was right, as I'm in the second year of my second-choice university now and having the time of my life. Lily.

It's impossible not to read anecdotes like this and feel elated and blissful, because you are reading about people operating on a higher, divine level of consciousness. You may also notice that the stories inspire a greater desire to help others because what you read renews your faith in human goodness. It's so easy to lose sight of that when we are constantly bombarded with news media highlighting the cruel and unjust ways people treat each other.

The sense of connection that kindness can inspire in us transcends those horrible feelings of separateness. Kindness links us together and reassures us that we are all part of the same consciousness – a heavenly concept that we'll explore in greater detail in Part Two. If you are kind, or someone is kind to you, there is a feeling of connection and resulting elation for you both. And if someone witnesses or reads about that act of kindness, the ripples of elation continue to spread and spread. And, as Sasha explains vividly in her NDE account below, heaven takes note of every kind thought, word and deed.

Taking a High Note

For the first time I saw what I had not seen before. I understood what thoughts, words and actions mattered in heaven and how material things, titles and money, were unimportant. Things you do from the kindness of your heart are all that count. As my entire life played out before me, I saw myself visiting a friend when she fell ill, being kind when others were unkind, speaking up for those who had no voice, helping a blind lady across the street, giving to those less fortunate than me, rescuing animals from cruelty, caring for family in times of need. I felt the instant impact of my thoughts, words and actions on others, and a lot of the things I saw I had no recollection of because I had done them thinking there was no audience or reward.

> I didn't realise that heaven was watching all the time and, as I hovered between life and death, I understood that love, kindness and compassion are the only currency in heaven. The greatest value is placed on the loving and kind things we do for one another.
>
> I also saw that every thought, word and action affected everyone and everything – even if it felt insignificant or inconsequential at the time. The little things were what mattered and I recognised that when I returned to earth. I always had a sense that I would return – I must not forget that. I consciously played the 'remember the small stuff' mantra over and over so that I wouldn't forget it because I knew my eternal life depended on it.

Every time you are kind, the effects are more far-reaching than you think. There is the heavenly effect on the person you help, the heavenly high you feel when you help, and then all the people who witness, hear or read about your kindness will feel a touch of heaven too. In this way, you play a truly essential part in lighting up the world – recreating heaven on earth.

8. GRATITUDE

The eighth Secret of Earth is **gratitude**.

People who have died and glimpsed heaven, or people who have had afterlife encounters, often write and tell me their experience heightened their gratitude for the gift of their life. There is a thankful light in their eyes – a light that shines directly from heaven.

PS: Thank You

PS: Thank you for understanding and not judging. I'd be honoured if you shared my NDE in a future book and happy to keep my first name. I know I told you that I really didn't want to come back when my little brother said it wasn't my time to pass over. I didn't want to come back because I was in a state of ecstasy. I felt loved as I have never felt loved before, and there was unspeakable beauty everywhere, rushing through me and all around me. Any words I use would fail to sum up the peace and joy I experienced. I think the closest word is bliss.

> Anyway, although I really didn't want to come back – and this is so contradictory but I believe it will make sense to you – I am so incredibly grateful that I was given another chance at life. There isn't a second of my life that goes by that I don't thank heaven for the opportunity to learn and grow spiritually on earth and help others learn and grow too. Every moment with my family is a treasured one, and I can't thank heaven enough for giving me more precious time with them here. I can't thank heaven enough for the miracle of this truly wonderful life I have. My NDE has taught me the meaning of gratitude. Sometimes I feel so intensely grateful to be alive in spirit I cry – again I'm being contradictory because it is what you might call 'happy crying'. I'm grateful and sometimes I don't know why. I just have that quiet feeling of calm and confidence, but not for any particular reason. Lara

The spirit within is always loving, kind, confident and forever grateful. Scientific research even proves the divine essence of gratitude. Studies have shown that people who cultivate an attitude of gratitude are happier and healthier than those who don't. They experience greater levels of joy and happiness, have more energy and enjoy closer relationships. So if you want to be happier and lead a more spiritual life, gratitude is clearly essential, and anything that increases your happiness brings you closer to heaven. This is because a full heart takes you from fear to love, from restriction to freedom, from death to life. When you are grateful for something, your ego, and accompanying voices of limitation and fear, diminish and open up the pathway to your soul.

Gratitude also brings your focus sharply to the present moment – the place where heaven manifests. The deeper your gratitude the more you see the world through angel eyes; the more your life resonates with the divine energy that permeates everything and everyone and, as these next two stories below show, the more you connect with and manifest the true essence of heaven to those around you.

Turn Around

I will never forget my sister's birthday because it was the day I died. I was in hospital for a routine operation but woke up the night before with violent pain. I rang a button to ask for some water and pain-relief pills but by the time they arrived I was struggling to breathe. I heard alarms ringing and the footsteps of people gathering around my bed. I heard one of them say my pulse had stopped.

Throughout I remained intensely aware of what was going on. I remember thinking it was my departed sister's birthday today and I hoped she was waiting for me on the other side. Then I thought about my husband and son and how they would be fast asleep not knowing what was happening.

I was dying but that seemed very trivial and all that mattered was the bright light ahead of me. I felt my body being sucked into the light. I say 'body' but I also saw my body lying on the operating table, so it was my spiritual body heading for the light. I was in the tunnel and at that point I knew I had died. I felt no fear or anxiety, just calm, and all the pain was gone.

Then I became aware of my sister in the tunnel with me. I felt a strong pull towards her but she blocked my progress – firmly but not aggressively. She didn't say anything, she just turned around and, as she did, I was shocked back into my body. My heart was beating again.

I was released from hospital ten days later. Doctors told me I had died and they fully expected to make the dreaded phone call to my family, but I had come back to life suddenly and dramatically. In the weeks that followed I got my strength back slowly but surely and, during that time, I knew that my death was going to be the beginning of a new way of life for me.

Up until my NDE I had always felt trapped by my life and what was expected of me but, from that point onwards, I made a promise to myself to focus on what truly mattered to me – my family, my dreams of running a pet hotel and, of course, my son. So I stopped chasing after people who were not committed to me and told the people I truly loved how important they were to me. I fired my nanny so I could take care of my son and organised flexi-time at work so I could pick him up from school. I couldn't give up my banking job because we needed the income, but I quietly began to put in place my dream of running a pet hotel. I'm not there yet but I have set the process in motion.

One year after my trip to heaven I have moved to a new house, found new friends, taken less pay so I can be there for my son and, in my spare time, my husband and I plan our new pet hotel business. I never forget how lucky I am to be alive. I live each day of my life with deep, deep feelings of gratitude.

I don't know why my sister refused me entry to heaven – perhaps because it was her birthday and she didn't want me taking the limelight! She was a bit like that. The most magical experience for me wasn't seeing heaven; it was that I have stopped feeling trapped by life or the expectations of others. My sister turned her back to me and I have never looked back either. I love my life and everything about it, and was prompted to write to you because yesterday my son's form tutor told me during parents' evening that she had seen such a noticeable difference in my son's behaviour since my hospital stay. She showed me an essay he had written for her about who he admired. Instead of music or sports stars my son had written about me. You can imagine how blessed and intensely thankful that made me feel. Fiona

Speaking Terms

There is an old saying that if you've forgotten the language of gratitude you'll never be on speaking terms with happiness. I couldn't agree more. I know this life gives us lots to despair about – and I have had more than my fair share of grief, especially when my father died suddenly last year and my dear husband six months after – but I don't see the point in wallowing in self-pity and resentment. Yes, I miss them both deeply, but I try to be thankful for the time I had with them. And now I'm thankful for their loving presence on the other side.

Last week I had this wonderful dream and in it my dad and my husband were fishing together, which is surreal because my husband hated fishing. In fact, they had once refused to speak to each other for two years because my husband was an animal rights activist, and even though Dad repeatedly told him the fish were always thrown back it made no difference. It made me feel so happy and grateful to see them together like this and on speaking terms again in the afterlife – and the more grateful I am for this beautiful message heaven sent me the better I feel.

Of course I'm human, and have my moments of moaning, but I try to keep them to myself and to learn from them. Being thankful just feels good, Theresa, and I think an attitude of gratitude rubs off on the people around you. I don't want to moan and complain and cry because that's not good for me, or the people around me, and it isn't the language of heaven. Ellie

Gratitude guidelines

I wanted to include a few gratitude guidelines here before moving on, because even though since ancient times spiritual teachers, prophets and gurus have constantly stressed that gratitude is the key to a spiritual life, few of us today realise just how important it is for finding meaning in our daily lives.

Try this exercise. For three weeks ask yourself each day what inspired you, what brought you happiness and what bought comfort and peace. Spinoza, the celebrated seventeenth-century philosopher, believed this exercise would bring us happiness and fulfilment and lead to profound spiritual advancement.

Psychologists believe it takes a minimum of twenty-one days to break or make a habit, so why not try this exercise for three weeks and make gratitude a habit? You will be surprised how good it makes you feel.

Each day, at a time that works for you, think about all the things you have to be grateful for and, with each new day, try not to repeat what you thought of the day before; think of something new. This exercise need not take more than a few moments, but in those moments consciously focus on your blessings. By so doing you also strengthen the power of Secret Number Five (Attraction) because when you put your focus and your energy on good things you invite the universe to give more good things to you.

Closely linked to gratitude, and perhaps even synonymous with it for spiritual development and power, is the feeling of awe. Along with counting your blessings you may also want to spend a few moments each day filed with a sense of awe and wonder. Think back to when you were a child and you experienced the world around you in an almost permanent state of awe. Find things in your day-to-day life that can make your heart and spirit sing. Perhaps a glorious sunset or sunrise, or other beautiful things in nature, or perhaps a piece of great music or art or even the wonders of modern technology – the internet, for example, or your mobile phone would be considered God-like five hundred years ago.

It doesn't matter what you feel a sense of grateful wonder for, the important thing is by tapping into feelings of veneration, wonder and respect you will step up a gear in your spiritual development and start to grow wings.

Chain reaction

Just as kindness is infectious, you should also remember the domino effect of gratitude. If you express your gratitude to someone, it makes them feel loved and special and they in turn make the people they encounter feel special and so on. Each moment in our day is part of a chain of events, and all our words and actions build on each other to shape the world.

The words 'thank you' said over and over again are a divine mantra bridging the gap between this life and the next. This spiritual law applies not just to those spoken or written 'thank yous', but also to the silent thanks we can say with our hearts for everything that is good and beautiful in our lives. The afterlife is always listening. A grateful, loving heart is the fastest and most direct and clear connection from earth to heaven that there is.

9. REVELATION

The ninth Secret of Earth is the power of **revelation**.

The secret of revelation is one that slowly but surely became clear to me while researching and writing about near-death experiences and afterlife encounters. I realised that it was not just the astonishing information the accounts contained that lit me up inside, but the fact that people were actually coming forward and openly talking and writing about heaven, often for the first time.

Angel talk

So many people write to me starting their letters by saying something along the lines of, 'I haven't shared my experience with anyone before', or 'People laugh at me when I talk about what happened so I've hidden it inside me all these years'. When I spoke to Anita Moorjani, one of the first things she said to me was that when she decided to write down her near-death experience for cathartic reasons, and emailed it to a website that published afterlife accounts, she was so embarrassed that she used a shortened version of her name so no one would recognise that the story came from her. It took at least six months for interested publishers to actually track her down because she'd not given her real name.

It breaks my heart every time I read or hear someone say they feel embarrassed talking about heaven and what really matters in this life. It breaks my heart because I have dedicated my writing career and much of my life to encouraging people to open their minds to the possibility that heaven is real, but how can we do this if people are too afraid or embarrassed to talk about it?

That is why, in each and every one of my books, I strongly urge readers to get in touch with me and share their stories. If permission is given, and word count allows, I publish them in my future books to share with a wider audience. This book is no different from any of my others, and I do hope you will get in touch with your insights or questions. I love hearing from you and, although it may take me a while to reply sometimes, especially if you write a letter, as email is faster, I will endeavour to reply to everyone who writes to me. Better still, message me on my Theresa Cheung Author Facebook page.

The reason I invite this kind of interaction is that I truly believe the more we talk about heaven and the world of spirit, the more real it becomes. Remember the fifth Secret of Earth is Attraction – what you focus on with commitment tends to manifest in your life – and nowhere is this more apparent than when you share your experiences and insights about the other side with other people. If you talk about the afterlife, write down your thoughts and stories and share them with others, you are making a commitment to their reality. With each afterlife thought, word, text, story, or message on Facebook, you are truly helping to reveal heaven on earth.

Gathered together

Ever since I can remember I've been drawn towards the world of spirit. When several of my angel books went on to sell strongly, my mailbox started to swell with remarkable stories from people all over the world. The great majority of these stories were positive and uplifting but, for the understandable reasons previously mentioned, the people who were reaching out to me had previously felt uncomfortable sharing their stories. It became abundantly clear to me that my calling was to gather them together and share them, along with my own experiences, in book form, so the world could open its mind and heart to them. I could see that I was gently but surely being led towards a journey of researching and gathering contemporary accounts of afterlife experiences from people who wanted to share them.

Every time I write a book with a heavenly theme, I'm deeply moved by the generosity of those who give me permission to share their stories with you. Some will stretch your belief or even shock you – and in some cases names are changed to protect identity – but I can assure you that to the best of my knowledge they are all the real deal. In fact, I never fail to be struck by the truth and honesty of the people who contact me. And as a mark of respect to this truth and honesty I have always shared my deeply personal spiritual journey with my readers.

This isn't because I think my story is particularly dramatic or worthy of special attention (far from it), but because I feel that in order to present, appreciate and interpret the stories of other people it is important for me to have had similar experiences myself, and also to understand them. That's important, so my readers can see who I am and where I'm coming from.

Standing up

Although I'm a contented spiritual writer now, this certainly wasn't the case fifteen or so years ago when I was establishing myself as an author. Back then, most of my books were in the field of health, education and popular psychology. It was important for me to retain the respect of the academic community that had nurtured my inquisitive mind, so I felt I had to be low-key and completely objective about my passion for the world of spirit. If I'm brutally honest – and I always am – I think a part of me was embarrassed about my spiritualist upbringing and was desperate to fit in and be accepted by my academic peers. However, as the years progressed, and I read countless afterlife stories and witnessed more and more paranormal experiences, I gradually stopped trying to fit in. I found the courage to stand by my beliefs and to reveal to the world who I truly was. I may have been losing some of my objectivity in the process, but I was standing out rather than blending in and gaining a sense of meaning, purpose and fulfilment through my writing that I'd never had before.

I grew to understand that, taken in isolation, my psychic experiences could perhaps have been explained logically, or dismissed as coincidence, but not when I put them all together and looked at the bigger picture. For example, was the voice I heard in my head at a busy junction the voice of my mother in spirit warning me to take the right path instead of the left, as I intended? After the birth of my daughter, and a period of post-natal depression, did a series of lucid dreams and divine signs pull me through? Was my recovery from teenage anorexia triggered by a supernatural ray of sunlight streaming through my window?

I have known so many moments when the veil between this life and the next has grown thin and, as I hit my fourth and fifth decades, I began to see with a clarity I had not known before. Heaven had been guiding me and reaching out to me all along, but I just hadn't been ready to hear or see the presence of the divine. It was as if I needed to reveal my experiences in book form to give me confidence to believe.

In the years that followed I went on to write more and more openly and honestly about my spiritual experiences, mixing my stories with those of my readers. Along the way stunning coincidences, lucid and profound dreams and other astonishing events continued to occur, as if to constantly reassure and remind me of the reality of the world of spirit and the presence of heaven on earth.

You are not alone

In the process of gathering stories from other people I uncovered something rather wonderful: I was not alone. All through my life I had felt different and like I didn't fit in, but the people writing to me not only had similar spiritual experiences to me, they frequently mentioned having similar highly sensitive and emotional or quirky personality traits. The resemblance was uncanny. It was like I was finding my spiritual family on earth.

Many told me they were deeply sensitive to their environments and the feelings of others. They had a deep connection with nature, beauty and animals, and violence and cruelty in any form was like an arrow through their hearts. For some, just seeing a TV report about an injustice or cruelty was enough to send them into the depths of despair. Others felt they had a passion for healing, helping or teaching, but weren't sure how to turn this calling into a reality. Religion was important for some people but, typically, they didn't find it totally fulfilling. Some talked about being miserable at school, and how in their adult lives this 'square peg, round hole' feeling continued, as they struggled with low self-esteem, depression, weight issues or relationship challenges.

In the majority of cases most people didn't claim to be psychic, or to have actually seen spirits, but they still believed they had experienced something supernatural. They believed in something but didn't know what that something was. Reading these stories was like reading my own heart and soul. I wasn't alone. For the first time in my life I felt I belonged. It was like coming home – heaven!

Comforted and curious to know more, I researched and stumbled on – or perhaps was guided to – the term 'highly sensitive person'. This is someone whose nervous system is so acutely attuned to their environment or the people they're with that they process information very deeply and are easily upset by insensitivity or violence of any kind. Loud noises, crowds, busy streets, stress, and even powerful aromas, can provide too much stimulation. The incidence of stress and depression is higher than normal among such people because they are easily overwhelmed by the world around them, often tending to shut down or withdraw. Then they wonder what is wrong with them, why they can't get on with everyday routines and challenges like everyone else.

Psychologists estimate that, if tested, as many as one in five people would be diagnosed with acute sensitivity. The term 'highly sensitive person' was coined in 1996 by Elaine N. Aron, Ph.D, who believed it was actually a genetic trait. In times past, people with high degrees of sensitivity to the world around them and within them may have found themselves in the position of shaman, healer or counsellor, mediating conflicts or bridging the gap between this world and the next. However, in today's increasingly commercial world, the appreciation of people with high levels of sensitivity has all but disappeared. In fact, they may often be considered odd or anti-social. Many are constantly told they are too sensitive, that they need to get a thicker skin or get over themselves or, worse still, that something is wrong with them.

The more I read about the highly sensitive personality, the more I began to recognise many of my own struggles and experiences, along with the struggles, insights and stories of the people writing to me. Digging deeper, I discovered that psychologists believe highly sensitive people can't change their natures, and shouldn't have to. There are many amazing traits that come with being sensitive, including a high degree of imagination and creativity, a love of peace and calm, empathy and compassion for people and animals, an intuitive approach to life and an idealistic view of just how beautiful the world can be.

Most significantly, though, sensitive-natured people tend to have a deep connection or fascination with the spirit world. They may not always be able to articulate it, but they have a strong belief that a spiritual force is at work in their lives. Indeed it could be said that developing spiritually is essential for their fulfilment and happiness.

How I wished I'd had access to this information earlier. How it would have helped me deal with my sensitivity and feelings of alienation when I was growing up. Just knowing that I wasn't alone, and that what I had been regarding as my weaknesses could be turned into my greatest strength, was incredibly reassuring. And this is when I had a light-bulb moment. Realising it was crucially important for sensitive people to develop spiritually, because if they didn't they could get easily hurt and disillusioned, my passion for gathering afterlife stories and sharing them with as wide a readership as I could find grew even stronger. I didn't want anyone to feel as isolated and out of touch as I had. I understood with absolute clarity that everyone who sent their stories to me was a piece of heaven talking to me about what really matters in this life and the next. I understood the awesome power of revelation.

From then on I included my contact details in all of my books. I believe that everyone who writes to me is helping to make the world a kinder place. I believe this because I believe in the power of revelation. In other words, the more of us who talk openly about heaven, the more real it becomes.

Books of revelation

Remember that fifth Secret of Earth (**Attraction**) – the more you think and talk about something or someone the more likely it is to manifest in your life – and it applies just as much to heaven as everything else. Therefore, the less we talk about heaven the less likely we are to see and feel it. So if there is one thing you take away from this book, I hope it will be to talk more about the world of spirit and to openly share your spiritual thoughts and experiences with others. Put your focus on the search for true meaning in this life and your chances of finding it increase dramatically.

Also, sharing your stories about heaven – either because you have direct experience of it or because you are in tune with the beautiful message of peace, love and hope that afterlife stories bring – will lead to greater acceptance of those of a sensitive nature. Instead of trying to change, or berating themselves for being too shy, emotional or spiritually inclined in a material world, highly sensitive people will know they are not 'weird' or alone. Hopefully this knowledge will help them find the confidence and courage to appreciate and develop their unique traits, instead of trying to deny or repress them.

In a world fraught with violence, noise, chaos and an increasing pressure to do everything faster and to have more and more material possessions, I believe sensitive, spiritual souls are needed by society more than ever. Indeed, revealing their stories and experiences points the way forward for everyone – inspiring others to also look within and discover the hidden forces behind their lives.

Your sensitive soul

In short, *you* – and your desire for a more magical, loving and peaceful world where heaven can be seen, felt and heard – are needed now more than ever. You may wonder how I can say this about you. How can I tell that you have a sensitive soul, or that your greatest longing is to catch a glimpse of heaven on earth? I know this because by some miracle this book found its way to you. Think about it. There are billions of other books, ebooks, magazines, newspapers, blogs, websites and so forth that your eyes could be resting on right now. I am absolutely convinced therefore that either heaven, or the piece of heaven inside you, guided you towards this very book. You are reading it because you are meant to be reading it.

And when you let heaven guide and inspire you in this way, you reveal the world of spirit and light the way for others. You become the divine word the world is longing to hear. Through you others can hear the voice of spirit and catch a glimpse of heaven on earth. It goes right past their doubts and fears and silently slips into their hearts. Then, one day, that voice will echo from deep within and speak to them, just as it is speaking to you now.

10. DEATH

The tenth Secret of Earth is **death**.

Our life on earth begins with the miracle of birth and ends with the miracle of death but we typically think of the latter as a tragedy. I pray this book will go some way to changing that negative perception.

So often, death is viewed as a defeat or failure. People talk about the departed as 'having lost the fight' or 'battled until the end' and so on, as if taking our last breath is a battle that is either won or lost. If we win we live, if we lose we die. We go through life fearing death and not wanting to talk about it, but death is just as miraculous an event as birth. Every NDE I have read proves this. In addition, when those who have crossed over to the other side come back to life, they come back with all fear of death gone.

The miracle of death

Scientists are not entirely sure exactly how death occurs, and there is as much mystery surrounding it as the mystery of birth, but whatever happens it is a miracle because, as every NDE account shows, in the world of spirit we simply don't die. It is important to point out, though, that the very real possibility of life after death has already been accepted as the ultimate truth of life by many religions and mystics from the beginning of time. In the words of Rumi, 'Death is merely extinguishing the lamp before the dawn has come.'

It has become abundantly clear to me that death is a miracle because it opens the gateway to life in spirit. It reveals the true nature and source of life and replaces limiting concepts of time and space with timelessness and the infinite. Ask anyone who has lost a loved one – but still feels their presence in ways beyond the reach of their five senses – and they will understand what I am saying here about death being the source of eternal life. They will know that death reveals the true meaning of the eternal. They will know that only through death can we know ourselves and others as having an endless existence beyond time and space.

Even the most sceptical among us cannot deny that true meaning can never be found in physical or material things. We all, regardless of whether we believe in spirit or not, sense the answer to the mystery of life lies beyond the stars and beyond the physical realm. The answer to the mystery of this life, and the end of all suffering and fear, can only be found in spirit and revealed through the miracle of death.

The following quotes express this eternal truth far better than

I can. Take your time to ponder them, as they can nourish your mind, heart and soul.

> *You would know the secret of death. But how shall you find it unless you seek it in the heart of life?*
>
> Kahlil Gibran

> *Do not seek death. Death will find you. But seek the road which makes death a fulfilment.*
>
> Dag Hammarskjold

> *Death is only an experience through which you are meant to learn a great lesson: you cannot die.*
>
> Paramahansa Yogananda

> *Life is a dream waking. Death is going home.*
>
> Chinese proverb

> *Seeing death as the end of life is like seeing the horizon as the end of the ocean.*
>
> David Searls

> *Death is our wedding with eternity.*
>
> Rumi

> *I have absolutely no fear of death. From my near-death research and my personal experiences, death is, in my judgement, simply a transition into another kind of reality.*
>
> Raymond Moody

Death is nothing more than a doorway, something you walk through.

Dr George Ritchie

Life goes on

Like childbirth, there are many different kinds of deaths – some are traumatic and painful, others are slow and involve a lot of suffering, some are peaceful and so on. It is a shame in many ways that we do not prepare for our death in the way we would prepare for the birth of a child. There are no natural death classes, as there are childbirth classes but, from my brief experience as a care worker witnessing thc passing of elderly people, I believe there are things we can do starting today to make that transition less painful. We can live our lives according to the Secrets of Earth with courage, heart, honesty, love and kindness, so that when our time comes we can look back without regrets. We can learn to trust our body and spirit to know what to do and, if there is any pain and fear involved, as in childbirth, we can find a way to move beyond suffering and focus on what lies ahead – the promise of an afterlife.

I'm certainly not advocating euthanasia here – as I believe every day we have on earth is a sacred gift to be cherished – but I do believe there comes a time, especially if the body is painfully ravaged and wasted by disease and age, to stop fighting and go quietly and gently into the good night.

Glorious awakening

Just as a baby forgets the trauma of birth, I know that in the next life my spirit will soon forget the trauma of dying. My death will be a glorious awakening to eternal life.

How can I be so confident that my life will go on? Part Two: Secrets of Heaven will try to answer that question and many more besides.

PART TWO

SECRETS OF HEAVEN

Heaven is a permanent residence. A place where we unpack our bags and stay for ever. What a glorious thought to wake up in heaven and realise it is home.

C.L. Allen

Thinking about heaven can inspire and encourage us to be more heavenly minded and realise that heaven is a real place where we're going to live.

David Brandt Berg

We cannot even begin to imagine how wonderful heaven is.

Catherine Pulsifer

Heaven, the treasury of everlasting life.

Shakespeare

Heaven is how we hoped earth would be.

Anon

No goodbyes

You're going to die. Perhaps not today or next year or in twenty years but one day your brain will stop functioning, your heart will beat its last, and you will stop breathing, for ever. Not trying to panic you here, just speaking the ultimate truth.

It makes uncomfortable reading, doesn't it?

For most of us, even those who believe in heaven, talk of death is depressing, but I hope what you read in the pages that follow will go some way to changing that perception. I hope it will show you that there is plenty of evidence out there to suggest that death is a miracle or, at the very least, make you wonder if death really is the end of everything.

If imagining your own death is uncomfortable enough, imagining that someone you love is dying is even more unbearable, but losing someone you love is a scenario we all have to journey through at some point in our lives. Although I had worked in a care home and seen many people die, watching my mother gradually fade away was a totally different experience altogether. With my belief in the afterlife you might have expected me to be better equipped to cope than most, but I didn't cope well at all. In fact, I went into denial.

Doctors told me my mother had a good year to live but she actually passed away within weeks of her diagnosis. During this time I prayed for a wonder cure, treatment or surgery. I tracked down clinics, researched alternative therapies and prayed with every fibre of my being for heavenly intervention. I longed for a miracle to allow my mother to live and to walk away from this nightmare, back into normal everyday life. I begged heaven for a miracle that would, against all odds, deliver her from the inevitable. I prayed for a miracle.

And a miracle is what I got, just not the one I thought it would be, as my mother died suddenly and prematurely. I wasn't with her when she died. She died alone. Even her doctor was surprised how fast it happened. I couldn't take it in at all. In the final weeks of my mother's life I hadn't been with her or been able to say goodbye, because I'd been spending all my time and energy searching the world for a miracle.

It cut me into pieces that I wasn't there holding her hand when she died. I was at work and had just hung up the phone after a very hopeful conversation with a holistic healer promising me great results with a combination of diet, herbal cures and Indian energy treatments. The practitioner said he would phone me back to check availability for his next treatment session. I picked up the phone full of hope, as the time on my watch was 11.11 (always a positive sign for me) expecting to get an appointment time. Instead I talked to a messenger of death.

A gentle voice whispered that my mother had passed away. I didn't know what to say in response, but after several moments of silence I said something truly bizarre: 'Thank you. Is the weather good where you are? It is raining very hard here.' I think I then went on to talk about a number of random and unconnected things, firing unrelated question after question I didn't actually want to know the answer to. Eventually the voice on the other end of the line said that they were really sorry but they had to go and did I want the number of a bereavement counsellor? I refused, saying there was absolutely no need for that as I was fine: my mother had terminal cancer after all, so this was hardly a surprise. I think I even laughed as I said it.

As preparations were made for the funeral I continued to feel numb and disconnected. There was so much to do and organise. My practical side took over but, as the weeks melted into months, the grief would suddenly hit me hard, like a stone shattering glass, and I would find myself sobbing uncontrollably, sometimes in public. Clearly I wasn't dealing with my grief at all, and one of the biggest problems was that I was stuck in the denial stage. I simply could not comprehend that my mother had gone – that her physical presence had left this earth.

I also hadn't given myself the chance to tell her all the things that I wanted to tell her. I hadn't expected her to cross over so soon. Because of this unfinished feeling, and the fact that there had been no goodbyes, I didn't want any reminders of her around me. Seeing her spectacles, rings, clothing and other personal items triggered unbearable pain and a sense of finality I could not accept, so I gave almost everything away to charity and kept just a few items: her hand mirror, the last book she ever read with her handwriting still in it, some pieces of jewellery, her spectacles and her diary. I put these items in a silver-coloured cardboard box and hid them under my bed.

Of course, the way I was dealing with the shock was a recipe for disaster and unsurprisingly it fast-tracked me to full-blown depression a year or so later. Looking back, how much better it would have been for me if I'd had some recognition of death as the miracle it is. Perhaps then I wouldn't have wasted the final weeks of her life chasing miraculous cures. I could have instead used the time for being with her, saying all I wanted to say, getting used to the idea that her physical presence was fading. Facing forwards rather than looking backwards.

How much better for me would it have been to understand that our lives on earth, everything in the universe and every moment, is a miracle and that death is part of the miracle of this life. How much better would it have been to grasp the present moment, so that my heart could understand and accept that the miracle I prayed for was unfolding in my mother's death. How much better if I had understood that there are no goodbyes – just new beginnings in spirit.

I'm aware that it's a huge leap, especially in today's society – which sees death as something negative and to be feared – to place death as a miracle alongside birth. To put death on an equal footing with birth is going to be very hard for most of us, raised to worship youth and beauty. We live in a culture that neglects and devalues the old and regards death as a biological disaster to be mourned or a failure to fight and live on. And yet the eternal and liberating truth is that the miracle of life includes the miracle of death. You can't have one without the other. I sincerely hope what you read here will encourage a more harmonious approach to the end of biological life.

This isn't to say you should stop searching for a cure or the best treatment for a loved one who may be suffering, or that crying is wrong. What I hope to do is encourage you to think about death as a part of the miracle of eternal life. This shift in perspective may help you cultivate a less negative reaction to the event of death. It will also prepare you for the transition to a new relationship with departed loved ones in spirit.

In addition, thinking about death as part of the miracle of life encourages us to celebrate and live every moment to the full, because we know that death is not the end of who we are. We are part of the natural world and, if you spend time in nature, you will see the dance of life and death in perpetual motion. Indeed it can be hard to see where one starts and the other finishes, as both are intertwined. Think of the plants we eat, and of sunlight and rain. When we pass we become all these things in the circle of life – or, as I call it, the miracle of life. We don't think of it as wrong for a plant to die to give us sustenance to live. We are part of the natural world and I believe human nature means just that – being part of nature.

Nature is not external to us. It is part of us. The more we lose contact with that, and the fact that life feeds on death, the more we lose contact with the intertwining relationship between life and death and the miracle of our ongoing existence in both this life and the next.

The countless near-death experience and afterlife stories I have been sent over the decades offer intoxicating proof that our consciousness most certainly goes on after the death of our physical bodies. These accounts provide evidence that death is perhaps the greatest miracle of all because in death our consciousness (spirit, essence, soul or life force) leaves our bodies and goes in pursuit of ultimate answers, joy and love. On this earth our spirit is concerned with earthly things but in the next life it is liberated and free to concentrate only on what is divine.

Death is therefore our golden opportunity to discover who we really are. If only I'd had this awareness when my mother died it would have sustained me and eased some of my suffering as I adjusted to the loss of her physical presence.

Time to believe

Of course, it isn't only anecdotal evidence that points to the very real possibility of an afterlife. There is a growing and compelling body of scientific evidence and verified experience out there.

In 2015 I had the privilege of interviewing a neurosurgeon who brought this sensational phenomenon firmly into the spotlight. It would surprise me a little if you hadn't read or heard of *Proof of Heaven: A Neurosurgeon's journey into the Afterlife*, which narrates Eben Alexander's astonishing journey to heaven while in a coma after a bout of bacterial meningitis. He is a courageous and eloquent spokesperson for the divine – a twenty-first century prophet. Here's the interview I did with him:

Dr Eben Alexander: Interview with the Prophet

Confidence in heaven

Why is *Proof of Heaven* so popular? The answer is simple: once you have read it you can have confidence that heaven exists because it is written by a neurosurgeon who had a NDE. In my previous book, *How to find Heaven: Your Guide to the Afterlife* (Simon & Schuster, 2015), I mention the massive popularity of Dr Alexander's book and suggest that it has been a catalyst for the sudden rebirth of belief in heaven in recent years. It is therefore a huge privilege and honour for me to be given the opportunity to talk to the man who has made heaven 'hot' again.

Like millions of others, I devoured *Proof of Heaven* when it was first published, and it was bliss to have an hour of Dr Alexander's time to ask him the questions I have wanted to ask for a few years. A little nervous, I start by telling him I'm a writer of spiritual books. I tell him I feel a bit of a lone voice sometimes here in the UK, as we can be a very cynical nation, and if you write about the afterlife, spirits and heaven you open yourself up to criticism. He jumps in right away with words of strength and encouragement and tells me we must all work together for spiritual awakening and I'm doing a great job. I'm comforted by his generosity and feel a glow of courage and inspiration. Dr Alexander is sharing a piece of heaven and offering me spirit. I feel blessed.

Spreading the word

Our conversation about *Proof of Heaven* now begins in earnest. What immediately strikes me is his astonishing eloquence; his ability to effortlessly use words to merge profound spiritual insights with complex scientific and medical terminology/theories and, in the process, make it all sound so easy to understand. He tells me that spiritual truth is extremely simple but religion and the material world have just over-complicated it. The spiritual writer in me is a little envious. Not only has this man actually stepped inside heaven, seen it, felt it, he also has a medical background to give scientific substance to his beliefs and, to top it all, a remarkable gift for language. I praise him for his eloquence. He is surprised and this genuine humility suggests to me that the good doctor has been so busy spreading the word these last few years, he has no idea he has actually become the word!

Dr Alexander explains that before his coma he was a regular speaker at medical events. He believes all that public speaking prepared him well for his true purpose in life, which is what he is doing right now – using words to tell us about the reality of heaven – something he says we already know but have just forgotten along the way. He believes nothing in our lives is truly random, and if we open our minds to the presence of the divine in our lives we will all find fulfilment, direction and bliss. He also believes that his distinguished career as a doctor was the perfect preparation for his vocation now, and frankly admits that one of the reasons the world sat up and took notice of *Proof of Heaven* was that he was a neurosurgeon – someone we normally think of as being sceptical and rational rather than spiritual.

He looks back on his life and sees the hand of heaven gently guiding his life and career choices, although he admits he certainly wasn't aware of this at the time and was, in fact, not deeply religious or spiritual before his NDE. He has no doubt he was chosen for his current role as a messenger from heaven – indeed, while he was in heaven, the divine, loving force told him that he must return to earth for this very purpose.

When Dr Alexander first woke from his coma he had no memories of his life as a neurosurgeon – earthly memories took about eight weeks to come back. All that felt real and alive to him was the spiritual world he had visited in his NDE. As I speak to him I can sense this is very much the case for him now but, despite this otherworldly quality, he is very engaged with the here and now. Three years on from the publication of his book he is busier than ever with a frantic schedule of lectures, talks and interviews (with the likes of Oprah Winfrey) as well as promoting his books and working on new projects.

Soul school

Inevitably I ask Dr Alexander what heaven was like for him. He describes it to me as an eternal place of butterflies, love, angels, music, telepathy, lost loved ones and bliss. He states that his NDE could not have been a dream or hallucination because his coma made his cortex non-functional – in other words, the human part of his brain was dead. His medical credentials give this claim serious respect, as it takes a lot of courage for a respected neurosurgeon with decades of experience to openly declare that consciousness is not brain. He must have known the negative reaction it would generate among his medical peers and, unsurprisingly, he has collected his fair share of fierce critics along the way.

There is not a hint of bitterness towards the sceptics who constantly hound him, though. Indeed, he insists they are actually playing an important part in the spiritual revolution that will one day light up the world. Every time sceptics disagree with him online or in books or go on the TV or radio to 'debunk' him, he says they may not realise it but they are encouraging people to talk about heaven and that is exactly what he wants. He wants us all to wake up mentally and spiritually and start asking deep questions of ourselves – to see that the old way of thinking about this life just isn't working any more; that religious dogma is restrictive, and science simply cannot explain consciousness. He wants us all to know that the material world and the voice of ego (fear) in our head are mirages distracting us from the eternal, loving reality of heaven that exists within and all around us, in both this life and the next. He sees this life very much as a place for our souls to learn and grow – a bit like 'soul school'.

Our conversation naturally turns to the eternal, 'Why do bad things happen to good people?' question. Dr Alexander reminds me that every tear we shed, every obstacle we face, and every cut to our hearts is an opportunity for spiritual awakening. Lots of people write to him during times of grief and loss, and he tries to answer as soon as he can. I can tell from the sound of his voice that he genuinely cares about every single one of his readers, and anyone who writes to him will get a heartfelt response, if not from him, then from members of his committed team. He is a firm believer in reincarnation, stressing repeatedly that, to him, it makes perfect sense. I'm reminded of one of my favourite quotes here: 'We don't go to heaven, we *grow* to heaven', and Dr Alexander agrees wholeheartedly.

Our consciousness never dies

Dr Alexander is at pains to point out to me that you don't have to almost die, as he did, to awaken spiritually. We don't all need that dramatic wake-up call. The divine spark of awareness is within each and every one of us, waiting for us to connect with it – and we can do that through meditation, or by recognising the presence of spirit in our daily lives in our own personal way. However, most importantly of all, we can do it by understanding the life-changing power of the message he is determined the world will hear: our consciousness never dies. NDE stories, like his, are absolutely crucial to this understanding because they demonstrate, along with phenomena like telepathy, psychokinesis, dreams, visions, afterlife encounters and angel experiences, that consciousness is a far deeper mystery than scientific materialism can ever explain.

Consciousness, as Dr Alexander puts it, is eternal and divine and all one. Space and time are illusions and this is something that Einstein figured out a century ago. (If you have read Dr Alexander's books, you will know that he is fond of quoting Einstein to illuminate his text.) The doctor explains that as long as scientists hold onto the idea that materialism can explain the nature of reality, and that the brain creates consciousness, they will never be able to explain the enigma of quantum physics or consciousness. There is, however, reason to be optimistic, as he believes there are a growing number of open-minded scientists and doctors out there, like him, who do understand, and this understanding will be at the forefront of the spiritual revolution he believes is happening right now. (Interestingly, he adds that, in his experience, nurses, the people who are most likely to be beside a person when they pass over, are way ahead of doctors in understanding that death is not the end. I could not agree more as, over the years, I have had countless letters from nurses sharing stories of death-bed visions/experiences with me – many of these stories formed the basis for *An Angel Healed Me*.)

See the light

Our conversation now moves to the feeling of unconditional love that Dr Alexander experienced when he was in pure consciousness or heaven. While he was there he knew he was loved, could do no wrong and had nothing to fear. For him one of the reasons there is evil in the world is that people don't love themselves and each other enough. They don't realise they are spiritual beings and we are all one. 'When you see the light,' he says, 'you realise that unconditional love of self and others is the secret of eternal life, the gift we can all experience.' For him hell does not exist: it is simply the absence of light and love. I could not agree more.

Talking to Dr Alexander is like taking a refreshing spiritual shower after a heavy, dreamless sleep. You feel alive and energised and emerge with clarity of mind and heart. Reading his books has exactly the same effect, so if you haven't read *Proof of Heaven* or *Map of Heaven* yet, then you really should. You may also want to visit his website www.ebenalexander.com or write to him, as I truly believe the man is a messenger from heaven. There is a name for someone like that – a prophet.

Dr Alexander would, again, probably be surprised and humbled if I called him that, because he is too busy right now writing, teaching, talking and lighting the way for his medical and scientific peers, but I believe in time that is what his followers will call him – an unassuming prophet, a divinely inspired messenger chosen to speak for and guide people to heaven.

Another pioneer leading the way in research into near-death experience is a visionary scientist called Dr Sam Parnia (former research fellow at University of Southampton and now at the State University of New York) who is convinced human consciousness can survive brain death, or the moment when there is no more activity in the brain. Since 2008, Parnia, an expert in resuscitation techniques, has gathered thousands of accounts of near-death experiences, or experiences which take place when a patient is brain dead.

In 2014, the results of his University of Southampton study were published. They provided the first conclusive evidence that consciousness exists for at least a few minutes after death. This gave even more substance to Dr Alexander's claim that he actually had proof of heaven. Approximately forty per cent of two thousand people who'd had cardiac arrests and survived at fifteen hospitals in the US, UK and Austria, who were interviewed by Parnia's research team, described some kind of awareness during the time they were clinically dead and before their hearts were restarted. One man even described leaving his body completely, and could detail the resuscitation room, the machinery in it and the nursing staff present at the time.

The brain is unable to function when the heart stops beating, so his description suggested some form of consciousness surviving death. Although many could not recall specific details of their NDE, common themes emerged. One in five said they felt an unusual sense of peacefulness, whilst nearly one third said time slowed down or speeded up. Some saw a bright light, a golden flash or the sun shining. Others said their senses were incredibly heightened when they 'died'.

Parnia believes many more people have had these experiences but their memory is blocked by drugs or sedatives used in the process of resuscitation. Countless people have reported NDEs, but until Dr Parnia's study there had been no proper scientific research into them and they had been dismissed as hallucinations. Parnia's study, published in the journal *Resuscitation*, has opened the door for further extensive research into proving that heaven is real. A new age dawns. Along with quantum physics allowing the possibility for the existence of the paranormal, science and spirit are finally beginning to merge. Exciting times lie ahead.

Another phenomenon that's hard for scientists to dismiss completely is the out-of-body experience, or OBE, when someone who is unconscious or on the brink of death is somehow able to float above their body in spirit, see what is happening to their body, and perfectly describe what is going on in the room.

Many NDErs mention seeing deceased relatives rather than people who are still alive. If the experience was an hallucination you might expect them to meet living relatives, but they don't report that to be the case. Also fascinating are the rare instances when a person meets a dead relative on the other side whom they did not know had died. This is what happened to Dr Alexander when he 'met' his sister. He did not know he had a sister, as he had been adopted and so had she. After his recovery he was shown a picture of her and recognised her instantly. There are also accounts of people accurately describing never-before-seen biological parents, and children talking about departed relatives they didn't know they had. Another compelling argument for the reality of NDEs is their hyper-reality and clarity. Hallucinations tend to be confused, and in time become faded, but NDE accounts tend to be vibrant and stay strong in the patients' minds, no matter how many years pass.

Another peculiar aspect of NDEs is how similar they are, regardless of a person's age, culture, religion, gender and beliefs.

Symptoms include: leaving the body; looking down and seeing one's self on an operating table or scene of an accident; watching medical procedures as doctors or paramedics try to restart one's heart; feeling drawn into a tunnel towards a bright light and feeling the presence of a higher power with angels, spirits or departed loved ones reaching out to them through the telepathic medium of unconditional love.

Even people blind from birth report the same sensation and, by so doing, appear to prove the unprovable. If such visions were the random firing of dying brain cells, then each person's visions should be unique to that individual. However, perhaps the most convincing evidence for me is that the great majority of people who have these experiences report them as being dramatically positive. They lose their fear of death and become more optimistic and happy, no matter what their personality was before they 'died'. For me, this is all the proof I need that they have indeed visited heaven.

This is all just the tip of the iceberg regarding evidence for life after death. None of it is one hundred per cent conclusive yet, but if you take just one thing away from it all it should be that the growing body of evidence for the existence of life after death means we should not fear death as much as we do. It very possibly could be the greatest miracle that will ever happen to us.

Crossing to the other side

A lot of people ask me what happens when you cross over to the other side. I haven't had direct personal experience of this, as you know, but the fact that research now shows these experiences happen when the brain has flat-lined or stopped is nothing short of a miracle. What all these stories reveal quite clearly and strongly is that when someone dies their consciousness goes on. They also give us some hints and clues about what happens as we cross over from being alive to the realisation that we have passed on.

When the heart first stops and the brain flat-lines it appears the dying person has no awareness of the fact they have died, but they gradually start to realise what has occurred. As they realise this, the physical world begins to diminish until everything becomes non-physical. This can happen gradually or it can happen by a sense of floating away from the body or looking down on it or a room or places they are familiar with. The dying person feels lighter and free of any limitation, yet there is awareness that the mind is alive. At this moment there is typically a sense of a divine presence clothed in light, or a feeling of overwhelming unconditional love that communicates telepathically to the dying person. Although a sense of 'I' remains, personality begins to fade and the 'I' longs to move forward to another level of existence.

What occurs in that level of existence differs dramatically from person to person, as you'll see in the stories that follow, perhaps suggesting that every day of our lives we create the reality of our afterlife with our own thoughts and feelings about what heaven might be like. Perhaps the images of heaven we see are the soul's way of helping us adjust to our new existence in spirit, or perhaps the afterlife is created in a consciousness that isn't in the brain but exists somehow outside ourselves.

But what is heaven like?

For Dr Eben Alexander, heaven was beautiful and complex: *'I had no language; all my earthly memories were gone. I had no body awareness at all. I was just a speck of awareness in a kind of a dark, murky environment, in root or vessels or something and I seemed to be there for a long time – years. I was rescued by this beautiful spinning white light that had a melody, an incredible melody with it that opened up into a bright valley, an extremely verdant valley with blossoming flowers and a just incredible, rich, ultra-real world of indescribable beauty.'*

As often happens, the truth of Dr Alexander's claims about his supernatural experience has been heavily criticised and it is not for me to judge here. I spoke to Dr Alexander and found his passion and eloquence to be genuine and believable but, at the end of the day, it is the message that is important rather than the messenger. Dr Eben's NDE has striking similarities to all the others uncovered by scientists like Dr Parnia and indeed records that stretch across the centuries, way back to the time of Plato. All these millions of accounts can't all be wrong. Something truly extraordinary happened to these people when they were close to death, and each of their stories provides a treasure trove of insight into what awaits us on the other side.

Every NDE story I receive is stunning and I wish I could publish them all, but here is a tiny cross-section.

Valentine's Day

It was 14 February 1989. I was twenty-three and I'd just been dumped by my boyfriend – on Valentine's Day of all days! I was crazy with anger and grief. My heart was broken. I took the day off work because I knew I'd be bursting into tears all the time. I spent most of the day wandering around aimlessly, fighting back tears. I didn't eat or drink. I just walked and walked for hour after hour.

The car was travelling at 45mph in a 30mph speed limit when it hit me. If I hadn't been so numb with grief I might have noticed it and reacted in time before it ran me over but I wasn't quick enough and my head and skull were crushed. I could feel my face swelling fast, and I could see in two different directions.

Someone yelled, 'Call an ambulance!' It seemed like only seconds and the ambulance was there. They started an IV and rushed me to hospital. We went in through Emergency and straight up to the operating room. Lying on the table, I saw the nurses and doctors with their backs to me, readying for the operation ahead. Then this strange feeling came over me and I told myself, 'Rana, you can just stop breathing.'

With a sudden whoosh, it was like I was on a super-fast elevator going up through a tunnel. Ahead only darkness, when suddenly there was a very bright light straight ahead of me. Then a sudden stop and I had this overwhelming feeling of total knowledge of everything that had ever happened, and everything that ever will happen. Every question I'd had in my life was suddenly answered. There was an intense smell, like the most fragrant garden imaginable. I heard (or felt) a voice saying, 'Rana, you know what's happening to you, don't you? I said, 'Yes, Grandma. I'm dying.' She then said to me, 'You shouldn't be dying. You have so much to do.' I then told her, 'I can't live without him,' and my grandma nodded and smiled at me, saying, 'You're strong without him.' She then told me to stop looking at the light.

I turned away from the light. I felt myself falling fast but gently down. It's strange, but I could actually feel my mother's love pulling me back to earth (even though she had no idea what was happening to me). I opened my eyes, and heard a nurse say, 'Doctor, she's breathing.'

I was in hospital for six months and had several operations to rebuild my face, but it wasn't just my face that was rebuilt after the accident; it was also my heart. I'd always doubted my ability to cope alone but my trip to heaven had strengthened me. Each time I feel that life is tough I go back to that moment when my grandma smiled and reminded me of my own strength. Yes, the old 'me' died on that operating table, but a stronger me was reborn. Rana

Nigel, who tells his story below, also feels that his vision of the afterlife was a blessing in disguise.

Rewind

For several months I'd suffered from severe pain in my chest and arms and foolishly I didn't go and see the doctor. I'd just turned thirty and didn't think I was a candidate for a heart attack. I was fit and healthy and led a crazy, fun-filled life. I had the car, the job, the money and the lifestyle. Sadly, my love of the bachelor lifestyle cost me my marriage. I had an affair and my wife divorced me after two years. We had a daughter and she went to live with her mum. I saw her once or twice a month, but didn't really feel I was cut out for fatherhood.

I was just recovering from a bout of flu when a friend asked me to play a game of squash. Foolish once again, I agreed, and after two games I was lying on the floor in the middle of the squash courts having a savage heart attack.

I must have lost consciousness. I felt drawn through this dark tunnel where there was light at the end. When I reached it, I was surrounded by light beings, many who had faces. One light figure started talking to me and told me not to be afraid, that he was an angel. He told me the angels would appear to me both in physical forms and in light bodies, showing me so I would not be afraid. He told me I would be sent back because there was a special plan for us, and this would be revealed to us later. I was not afraid, for the warmth of the light and the light bodies around me were full of love, giving me a sense of security. Suddenly I was back in my body but I couldn't open my eyes. I saw paramedics put me on a stretcher and bundle me into an ambulance. I saw the paramedics trying to revive me.

Then I remember being surrounded by bright lights. I felt so happy. I remembered everything about my life from the very first spark. I relived every tear, every sigh and every kiss. I remembered what my purpose was on earth. I remember wondering why I spent so much of my time on earth fretting about things that didn't matter.

I don't remember much else, except that I was filled with joy and happiness. I didn't want to leave but I knew I had to go back. Then I saw my daughter crying because, once again, I'd cancelled my weekend with her due to work commitments. I asked the angels if she was OK and they said she was fine but she was upset with me. I could feel her hurt, her loss.

In the next moment I was back in my body in hospital. I felt my body filling with warm, intense light and then it was gone. The feeling was so full of love that I felt safe and secure. I opened my eyes and a doctor asked me if I was OK.

I learned a lot that day about life and death. Seeing the bliss that awaits us after death touched and enriched my soul. I see my daughter twice a week now and am learning to be a better dad. I'm no expert, and I'm never going to win a Father of the Year award, but my experience showed me that in the realm of the angels there is only love and truth, and any act that is thoughtless or selfish or hurts someone else is relived. That's why I now always take a moment to reflect on my actions and words, to make sure they come from a place of love and compassion – not just for myself, but for others.

Elaine also believes her 'death' was a miracle.

The Luckiest Woman Alive

I don't want to go into the details of why I nearly died, as some things are too personal, but I want to tell you what happened. I remember hearing a man saying that he could not find my pulse. I remember feeling surprised because I had never felt more alive. For the first time in my life I was bursting with energy and a sense of purpose. I couldn't hear, see or talk to anyone, but it didn't matter. I didn't mind. I just let things go. Next thing I notice is that I'm not alone. I also felt like I was where I needed to be and there was a sense of expectation, like the moment before you unwrap a present. There was also no concept of age or time. Everything – my past, present and my future – was there with me.

Within moments I experienced this eruption of light from within me and around me. From not seeing or hearing anything at all, suddenly I could see and hear everything. The light was so bright but my eyes did not burn. I instinctively knew that the light was love, divine love.

I've never believed in God, and I've never been religious, but I recognised this as sacred. This divine light was directed at me and coming from me. Through the light I had awareness and knowledge. It wasn't like understanding maths or a different language, but understanding the meaning of life. The answers to age-old questions suddenly became obvious. I knew who I was and why I was here, and I knew that the purpose of my life was to love. It was like I was remembering things I had always known but had forgotten. It seemed ridiculous that I had not worked things out before.

Then my euphoria was broken and I knew I had to return to my life on earth. I didn't want to but I knew I had to. I landed back in my body. Later I learned that I had died twice on the operating table. Doctors told me I was the luckiest woman alive. I agree with them, but not in the way they think. I'm not lucky to be alive, because I know that I never died and never will. I'm lucky because the old, confused, purposeless, frightened me died on the operating table and a stronger me was reborn. My experience changed my life forever.

All these accounts suggest that in heaven we reunite with loved ones and our spirits try to send love and guidance to our loved ones still on earth. They also indicate that life on the other side is joyous, loving, beautiful, peaceful and magical beyond belief and everything and everyone is interconnected and given life by the power of love. You may want to refer back to the guiding and inspiring light of these stories as the final Ten Secrets of Heaven are revealed in the pages that follow.

Time and time again I am asked what heaven is actually like, and I hope the stories above and the remaining secrets that follow will give you some indication or sense of what to expect. As the stories differ greatly in the details, and the world of spirit is beyond human description or comprehension, it's impossible to be precise when attempting to answer the 'what is heaven like?' question, but certain consistencies can be detected and, from the countless accounts sent to me over the years, here are ten definite similarities (or secrets) of heaven that I've been able to pinpoint.

Discover those secrets for yourself and, hopefully, you will get a very real sense of what your life in heaven will actually be like and what it is like for those you have loved and lost. Hopefully you will start to see death, if not as a miracle, than in a totally new and brilliant white light.

1. AWARENESS

The first Secret of Heaven is sensational **awareness**.

You are spiritual beings having a human experience, not human beings having a spiritual experience.

Anon

I was about seventeen years old when I first really heard the words above. I had, of course, heard them many times from my mother and in the numerous spiritualist meetings I attended, but they were just words. I didn't start trying to make sense of what they truly meant, however, until my teenage years.

A school friend of mine had recently lost her father due to a surprise heart attack and she was devastated. I wanted to say something to her that would help ease her pain. I couldn't bear seeing her hurting so much but I struggled to find the right words. I remember sitting beside her in silence and a part of me, I'm ashamed to admit, longing to escape the claustrophobic and intense atmosphere of grief. I fought that feeling and begged for heaven to give me some words and then, before I knew it, I told her that her father was alive in spirit because we are spiritual beings having a human experience and not the other way around. For a brief moment – and it was truly brief – I saw her face shift from twisted torment into cautious hope. It was just a flicker of joy, and the moment soon passed, but I have never forgotten it because it felt like a message from heaven that I was on the right track. I was telling her what her heart and spirit needed to hear. It was telling her that we don't die.

Put simply, the reason NDE stories blow our minds and fill us with a sense of hope and wonder is because they illustrate the very same message, of life being eternal. When we die, we leave our bodies behind and discover that our physical lives were never what defined us or who we really are. Our body was simply the clothing for our spirit or soul. Our spirit survives death and continues a new life on the other side. In this respect, heaven is our true home and earth a place we travelled to for a visit. The first secret of heaven, therefore, instantly reveals itself with astonishing clarity that the end of our physical lives is a gateway to our true home – heaven, for we don't die. We are eternal.

Truly believe

> *After you die, you wear what you are.*
>
> St Teresa of Avila

The moment you truly believe in your eternal spirit, in the reality of heaven, is the moment your entire perspective on life changes. Most of us have flashes or moments of divine illumination in our earthly lives but they are rarely sustained. For example, we may sense the presence of a departed loved one or grasp a moment of transcendence when we gaze in awe at a beautiful view, or lose ourselves in glorious and timeless happiness when we fall in love. All these blissful experiences give us tantalising glimpses of heaven on earth, but then the routines, responsibilities and questions of earthly life take over and we lose sight of our eternal existence. Once we cross over to heaven, however, that peak or transcendent feeling never fades because we know with absolute certainty that life is a continuum. We realise that consciousness survives, and death is simply a transition to another form of existence. We realise that we still exist – we sense and feel and think as we did before but we are operating on another level of existence.

Understanding our life as an eternal state has tremendous consequences and the so-called 'life review', when your entire life is played back to you in heaven, that many NDE stories mention, underlines this. The concept of life as a continuum jolts us into an awareness that every thought we have, action we make or word we say really, really matters. Everything matters. Nothing in this life or the next can be trivialised. There is always that famous saying, 'You only live once', which we quote to encourage us to live life to the full – and I applaud that – but sometimes we use it as an excuse to do unkind or selfish things. Perhaps it would be better for us to reflect instead on the eternal meaning of our lives.

One enlightening way to fully comprehend how the concept of eternal life changes us is to become conscious of the fact that everything you do will be taken note of and reviewed in heaven. Think of your every word and your every action as reviewable. How would your interactions with others, even the person who serves you coffee, change? Try it for a day, starting from tomorrow, and you will know that believing in heaven changes everything in your life for the better.

The illusion of time

In heaven we understand that life never ends. We also learn that the concept of time as we comprehend it simply does not exist. Time is not real. Time is a creation, an illusion. There is no time as we experience it when we are alive. Our souls exist beyond and outside of time.

Einstein suggested that time only exists to stop everything happening at once. What he meant was that the concept of linear time (things happening one after the other) is a concept created by our minds to allow things to happen in an orderly manner. Without a system of measuring time there would be chaos. His theory of relativity showed that time is not constant or linear but can be changed or altered by the speed and direction of a moving object.

The awareness of time as being fluid, of operating differently outside of consensus reality, can have a tremendous impact on the way we live our lives. The realisation that, from the perspective of heaven, our life on earth could be over in the flash of a second, and that events may be happening at blinding speed or occurring simultaneously (but be slowed down and ordered in our minds, as we live in a physical rather than a spiritual universe) helps us to understand that a ninety-year lifespan on earth may take place in the blink of an eye in spirit. So perhaps the reason some of us don't receive any sign, or feel a strong sense of connection with departed loved ones, is because the departed feel they have only been gone a few moments, or have not left at all, and they know you will be together with them again in the blink of an eye.

Life is death

We fear death because we think it is the end of everything but this couldn't be further from the truth. NDE stories show that death is not an end but a part of life. If you think about it, you are dying every single moment of your life in that you leave behind moments that you can never revisit physically. The years fall behind you just as autumn leaves fall off a tree. The process of growing older is not something we typically fear but learn to accept, embrace even, and I hope awareness of your eternal life in spirit will remove any fear of death you have and replace it with calm and loving acceptance.

Only by losing your fear of death can you live life with true passion and commitment. Living your life anxious that your days are numbered will numb any passion for life you have, but when you understand that you are an eternal spiritual being suddenly you will feel more alive than ever before. Losing fear of death is, of course, easier said than done but perhaps this little visualisation exercise might help.

Think about yourself as a child. Now think of yourself as a teenager or the person you were ten or twenty years ago. Now think of who you are today. The child isn't the person you are now, so where has that child gone? That child was you with a different body and mind, but now that body and mind have, in essence, passed away or 'died' and been replaced by who you are now. This process happens at every age and stage of our lives, even each day and from moment to moment. So which 'you' is going to go to heaven? The self that was you as a child or the person you were aged twenty or the 'you' that lived yesterday or the person you are today?

What I'm trying to say is that your mind is constantly being reborn with thoughts and feelings as you age and your body is constantly changing and renewing itself. This doesn't stop you – your essence – from going on, from continuing, though. Every single second you are dying and recreating yourself. What I'd like you to do here is see yourself without being attached to any age or moment in your life. I'm trying to get you to observe yourself independent of your body and mind – to acknowledge the spirit in you that has always been constant, regardless of your age. This is the part of you that lives for ever. This is the part of you that goes to heaven.

You are not your body. So when you eventually die it will not be your soul leaving your body but your body being left by your soul – much as it has been doing all your life. Your soul is just moving forward into a new level of existence, as it has always done, and once you know you are eternal and unchanged in spirit then you have absolutely no reason to fear death or to doubt that you will see your loved ones again in spirit.

Death is life

Although I have never been to heaven, from what I have researched death very much seems like growing into a new form in a different place in space and time. (Some people talk about seeing their life flash before their eyes with complete understanding of each choice ever made before this transition to spirit occurs, but this is not the case for every NDE.)

Awareness that you are a spiritual being having a human experience, and that in the midst of life we are already in death, conquers all fear of death as an ending or void of nothingness. It will help you confront your own mortality. If you are ever in the privileged position to spend time with a dying person who is anxious and afraid, you can in gentle ways reassure, comfort and support that person with your new-found understanding. You could talk to them about their life and what filled them with feelings of pride and joy. You could encourage them to discuss any regrets they may have, and by so doing help them let go of those regrets. You could ask them how they feel about moving to another level of existence and tell them there is no need for sorrow and that they deserve to find peace. You could encourage them to become consciously aware of what is happening to them rather than diminish any physical life they have left with fear, guilt and denial.

Of course, talking about death is always going to bring up feelings of anxiety and uncertainty, because death is the great unknown, but if you can connect yourself and others to an awareness that death is a natural part of your life, and life is a natural part of your death, and the eternal 'you' will remain unchanged by death, then you will have discovered the first secret of heaven – the foundation stone of the afterlife.

> *I'm not asking you to believe anything. I'm simply telling you what I believe. And I have no idea what the next life will be like. Whatever I saw was only from the doorway, so to speak. But it was enough to convince me totally . . . that our consciousness does not cease with physical death; that it becomes, in fact, keener and more aware than ever.*
>
> George Ritchie

2. PRAYER

The second Secret of Heaven is the transformative power of **prayer**.

The measure of our prayer is the measure of our power.
Andrew Murray

NDE accounts reveal the miracle-making potential of prayer both in heaven and on earth. Along with total awareness that death is an illusion, the stories also teach us loud and clear that prayer is a super power that connects earth to heaven and heaven to earth. Heaven hears our prayers, and when we reach heaven we witness prayers and intentions becoming reality. We finally comprehend that prayer is the most powerful tool in the universe.

Here are some stories to illustrate the mighty power of prayer. The first two are well known and the last two were sent to my angeltalk email but, famous or not, they all reveal simply and clearly the astonishing power of prayer:

Prayers Gave Me Energy

I moved down through great walls of clouds. There was a murmuring all around me, but I couldn't understand the words. Then I realized that countless beings were surrounding me, kneeling in arcs that spread into the distance. Looking back on it now, I realize what these half-seen hierarchies of beings, stretching out into the dark above and below, were doing. They were praying for me. Eben Alexander

In the distance a gentle wave swelled up, moving across the ocean of light toward the point of perspective assigned to me. As it arose, I became aware that this wave was the concerns, prayer and emotions being streamed toward me from hundreds of people I knew in this life and from many others who had only heard about my situation ... It was made known to me that this was consciousness creating form through intention. Ned Dougherty

I could hear all the prayers and thoughts of all the people that loved me. There were fewer voices than I thought there might be but the voices I heard from my wife, children, family and a few friends were deeply beautiful and filled my heaven with love. Theresa, I could hear their thoughts and prayers as if they were right there with me. Anthony

The being of light told me every one of my prayers had been heard. I was also told that prayer groups were incredibly powerful – more powerful than leaders and politicians, and the future of the world could depend on them. I truly believe after my experience that our conscious thoughts and intentions and prayers create some kind of energy field and if something happened to me again I would give prayer the first not the last chance. If someone I loved was in trouble, I would try the conventional route, of course, but I would also bring faith healers into the picture. I would give prayer and miracles the first chance because I have seen that the entire universe is one huge miracle and I am a part of that and so are you. Elizabeth

Feel the force

Prayer is a powerful force. I think many of us underestimate just how powerful it is but NDE stories show that in heaven prayer has the first, last and everything word. Prayer can create miracles and bring healing and light but few of us truly believe that. If only we knew how powerful prayer can be, our lives would be transformed and we would not feel so helpless and alone.

Prayer connects us directly to heaven. Every time you pray your intention flies to heaven at breath-taking speed. Your prayers for yourself and others are always heard. Sometimes on earth we feel helpless, and that the only thing we can do is pray, but now that you know your prayers are always heard praying should not be the last resort but the absolute first thing you do.

Have you ever felt a surge of strength, comfort and peace when someone tells you that you are in their prayers? Even though no one is exactly sure how it works, research suggests there is real power in prayer. Research in some hospitals has shown that patients who were prayed for have faster release times.

The world is full of injustice, poverty and violence and, like many people, I often wish I could make a difference. Whenever possible I try to contribute money or time as a volunteer, but my budget is often too tight and my schedule too full. I used to feel as if there was nothing I could do, but reading stories of people who have crossed over to the other side has taught me that there IS something incredibly powerful that I can do – I can pray.

Praying, of course, doesn't always bring the answers or results we hope for. Some painful experiences are important lessons for the soul, and why terrible things happen to decent or innocent people is beyond our limited comprehension, but if we pray for what is best for us and for others, heaven will be listening by helping us find the inner strength to pull through. Praying for others strengthens the power of heaven to offer them healing, courage and comfort. Talk to people who have experienced personal tragedy or survived disaster and, more often than not, you will find that the trauma has helped them focus on the essentials in life and what really matters; the priceless gifts of health, of love and of life. Talk to anyone who has been close to death and they will tell you that when they thought their time was up they prayed.

One potent way to acknowledge the existence of heaven is to make prayer a significant and rewarding part of your life. Ask heaven for help, support and guidance. Pray with confidence, enthusiasm and trust, ready to love more deeply and learn more clearly. Don't ever feel unworthy in any way. Yes, there will always be people whose need is greater than your own, but in heaven the love is limitless and without bounds.

Be aware that heaven can answer prayers in any number of ways. Sometimes this happens in the form of a dream or a person appearing in your life at exactly the right time, or in meaningful words that seem to speak directly to you. It may respond in the form of a still small voice from within that speaks with gentle certainty when all around you there is chaos. It can also make its presence felt in sudden flashes of insight when you inexplicably understand or know something with absolute clarity. Never ignore those gut feelings or light bulb moments, as they could transform or even save your life. And sometimes heaven can answer your prayers in the form of a remarkable coincidence; an astonishing turnaround of events that takes your breath away.

The details of how, where and when you choose to pray is insignificant; simply believing in heaven and the power of prayer to reach heaven is all that's needed. So if you are ready to open your heart and invite the magic to come in, let the praying begin. Heaven hears both the prayers we say out loud and the silent prayers in our hearts, so don't feel you have to pray formally. There is no right or wrong way to pray. Spirit hears our voice in any form; not only as formal prayers – in the sense of bended knees and head bowed – but also the heartfelt prayers we don't even realise we are saying. I'm talking about your thoughts and intentions here.

All in the mind

Growing up in a family of spiritualists, prayer was an integral part of each day and night. The Lord's Prayer, for example, was engraved on my heart, as I'm sure it was for many people. Yet my early years of praying didn't sustain me and, as the years melted into each other, I parted company with the practice, especially as my distance from organised religion broadened. My thirst for spiritual fulfilment continued but I didn't realise that the thing I was unwittingly ignoring was one of the cornerstones of a spiritual life – prayer.

As has happened many times, it was my readers and the amazing stories they sent to me that helped me remember and reconnect with the true power of prayer. Many talked about their prayers being answered during a time of extreme crisis or grief. Even if the word prayer wasn't used, they talked about a heartfelt intention or desire made manifest in an extraordinary heaven-sent way. The stories refocused my mind on prayer and I set out to investigate, so I could write about the practice in an informed way in my books. What I uncovered was stunning, as I had no idea there was such a multitude of astonishing research out there with the words 'wilful and conscious intention' often used to describe the wide-ranging medical, psychological and spiritual applications of prayer. These words really spoke to my mind and my heart as they suggested the conscious (aware) use of thoughts or mind power to influence things. In other words, prayer.

The more I looked into the power of prayer the more I understood how it is possible to take responsibility for ourselves and our lives through a spiritual practice. I also realised that prayer does not have to be the traditional 'down on your knees, hands together' formal recitation of set words, but that it also encompasses our focused thoughts and intentions, and that meditation too is a form of prayer. I understood as I had never understood before that what happens in our lives, or what we decide to do with our lives, is never as important in the world of spirit as the reason why we do things or the intention behind them. NDE stories taught me that our intention is how our lives on earth will be measured on the other side. What kind of person were we on the inside?

Once you truly understand the incredible power of prayer your life will never be the same again. You will realise that you are not a victim of circumstances but can instead take control of your life by appealing to the universe to influence your experiences. In addition, prayer helps open our minds and hearts to the awesome beauty of the world we live in; the more we focus our thoughts on positive, healing things, the more we start to catch glimpses of heaven on earth everywhere.

Creating heaven one thought at a time

Quantum studies may offer some kind of explanation for the power of prayer, as they suggest that everything is energy or pure potential and the universe is simply a movement of this energy. The only difference between you and a butterfly, for example, is energy distribution, vibration, frequency and content. What sets you apart from a butterfly or a plant, however, is that you have a nervous system with the potential and capability to become aware of the energy that manifests as physical form. We experience this energy as feelings, desires, thoughts, intentions, beliefs, memories and instincts. Seen in this light your body and mind are not separate from the universe but a part of the universe. And not only can you become aware of the energy that manifests as you, it is also possible for you to change or alter it so that things manifest in your life.

Pretty amazing? You may want to take a few moments here to put this book down and reflect on the power of conscious intent or prayer, because what I am suggesting is that whatever you think deeply about or pay attention to will become stronger in your life, and what you don't pay attention to will fade away. If you build on the knowledge gained from the first secret of heaven – awareness of your true nature as pure spirit – and you carry this awareness with you at all times and focus with intent on what you want to manifest in your life, the chances are you will start to get what you wish for.

Letting go

I'm aware this sounds deceptively simple – wish for something hard enough and you will get it – as we all know this is rarely the case in life. Our dreams are often shattered and bad things happen to good people and often it feels that our prayers are not answered. How does the power of prayer resonate with this harsh truth of life? What I have learned over the years is that it has to have something to do with the paradox of longing for your heart's desire but then letting go of any attachment you may have to the result. Many people just aren't able to do that 'letting go' bit effectively.

Sounds confusing but it really is fairly simple. You don't stop desiring something but you detach yourself from the outcome. You may well have experienced this heavenly secret in your daily life: the moment you stop wanting something really badly and say, for want of a better word, 'Sod it, what will be, will be', is often the moment it starts to manifest in your life. This was the case with my relationships. In my early to mid-twenties I longed for a boyfriend but every relationship I had was short-lived and toxic and then, as I approached thirty, I decided to focus more on loving myself and to stop trying so darn hard to find my soul mate. Within months of doing that I met my future husband.

So, to truly harness the power of prayer you need to detach from the outcome of your prayers. Attachment is based on fear and lack of self-belief. If you are attached to worldly things, or the love and approval of others, or a certain outcome, then you will feel empty inside because you are focusing your intention and trying to seek security in things or people outside yourself, not inside yourself where the true potential for wealth, security and comfort lies. Sometimes you may want something so much and not get it and sometimes you may have all the right intentions and things go horribly wrong. What is going on here?

Sometimes we confuse happiness with feeling good. Happiness refers to things we think will make us feel good – more money, a sports car, a dream house and so on – but feeling good is a state of contentment, a quiet sense of wellbeing that comes from within. Sometimes, for reasons we may not understand, what is best for our wellbeing is to experience difficulties and loss, so that we learn and grow as spiritual beings. Sometimes the route to wellbeing takes a path through the darkness. We all go through tough times – whether in our relationships or because of illness or loss or through anxiety and depression – but by learning to let go and bravely keep going we begin to understand and see what we need to see and learn as spiritual beings. We can then rise above traumatic situations, leaving our fears and self-limiting ways behind, and reach a higher spiritual place.

Each one of us has our own unique path and sometimes, to grow as an individual, we need to walk through challenging times. If we can emerge from the darkness with a deep trust in the forces of creation, of which we are a part, and an awareness that we are not alone, and every thought and feeling we have is a part of the interconnectedness of things, we are in a state of bliss. We know deep down that everything we experience teaches us something valuable and helps us grow. By staying calm and treating triumph and disaster just the same, as the famous Kipling poem 'If' says, we are on the right path.

Detaching or letting go of external validation can be frightening at first. You may feel uncertain and unsure, but that uncertainty is a step in the right direction because you are putting your trust into the spiritual powers of the universe. You are keeping your mind open to possibilities. This doesn't mean you don't set goals or have a plan. Of course you do, but you allow yourself the possibility of changing direction in the pursuit of your goal. You don't shut out possibilities and you don't force things: you stay alert to opportunities. And if problems, disappointments, challenges or obstacles cross your path, you don't see them as problems – you see them as opportunities for a higher or greater purpose.

In short, thought that is intentional or directed harnesses spiritual power, but to manifest that spiritual power you need to detach yourself from the outcome – state your intention and then 'let go' and trust the universe to fulfil your spiritual needs. You can call this prayer or meditation or wishful thinking, but whatever you call it why not give it a try? You will soon discover the second secret of heaven, the power of prayer, points you in the direction of spirit.

And if all this wasn't awesome enough, I'll finish this section with another incredible thought from Milton's *Paradise Lost*.

Which way I fly, myself am heaven . . . or hell

There is a very real possibility that the heaven we experience is created by our prayers; our own thoughts and feelings. This is certainly the sense I have from the incredible people who have written to me about their near-death experiences and the frequently reported 'life review' – where a person's life is replayed for them to watch in heaven. Here are some extracts:

> In heaven I watched the movie of my life in sensory detail – everything was there in an instant and in panoramic memory. I felt all the emotions of my life, both happy and sad. I also felt what emotions I had inspired or provoked in other people. If I had made someone feel happy I felt that joy, and if I had been selfish or rude or hurtful I felt their pain. Nothing, even trivial things and thoughtless acts or words, were missed

out. I also felt sadness for every failed resolution or dream I had not accomplished. I'm telling you, Theresa, heaven notices everything, and I mean everything. Sonia

In the review of my life something really stood out and it was something I had long forgotten. It went right back to when I was aged eleven or twelve. I had been a bit of a bully at school and I used to tease this boy (he had a lazy eye) mercilessly. I never hit him or anything, it was just verbal, but I think I picked on him for over a year. In my review I felt the pain and alienation of that boy. I saw him at home in his garden with his family and how the pain I had caused him sent out negative energy to his mother, father and sister, and even to the flowers in the garden and the birds in the sky. This has taught me that everything in the world is alive in some way. Nothing is not alive. Tony

I saw in my life review that anything kind or loving I had done I had also done that for myself. Likewise if I hurt someone I had hurt myself. Does this make sense? I experienced my life again not so much from my point of view but from the point of view of others and how the environment around me experienced it. It became startlingly obvious that every thought, feeling, word and action affects others; trees, plants, animals too, and the entire universe. In my review I was not judged by any being of light or by anyone or thing. I was judged by myself but, as my ego had been left behind on earth, I couldn't hide any truth about myself from the light. This has taught me that on earth many of the things we think are important – career, money, status and so on – are not important at all in the world of spirit. It is often the insignificant things that matter. Tracy

All these stories indicate that if you have caused others pain in your life you will, in heaven, feel that suffering and pain. This isn't 'punishment' as such, but so you can learn from your misguided ways and evolve into a higher spiritual being. It seems therefore that you are quite literally, in every moment of your life, creating the afterlife you will experience on the other side – not just with your thoughts, desires and heartfelt intentions but with every word and deed.

What an awesome and potentially life-transforming thought!

> *Many NDE accounts talk about a life review and an accounting of experiences the soul had during life on earth. There is no punishment – more a soul education and repair when a soul will experience the suffering it caused and through that experience grow in understanding and move towards healing.*
>
> Anita Moorjani

3. CHOICE

The third Secret of Heaven is the amazing power of **choice**.

> *Heaven is a choice you make, not a place you find.*
>
> Anon

Many of us go through our lives feeling like victims of our circumstances or personality and that we have no choice. But what becomes immediately apparent from reading NDE accounts is that the life we have on earth is a choice that our souls or spirits, or the eternal part of ourselves, have made. There are specific lessons about love, fear, loss and calm that we need to learn on earth in our physical form that we can't learn in spirit, and so we choose to be born so we can evolve spirituality.

This theme, that our life is a school for our spirits to progress, comes up in a number of NDE accounts. What Tim narrates below is a classic example.

Love Lessons

> I know without any doubt that there is a meaning to my life and, as a result, I live every day with purpose and conviction. I have this conviction because in my NDE I understood completely that the physical world is a place for our souls to grow and learn. I also learned that life on earth is a tremendous privilege and opportunity for our souls, because it's easier to grow spiritually on earth than it is in heaven. On earth we are given a huge range of opportunities to experience different kinds of love – love of child, parent, partner, friend, pet, the natural world and so on – whereas in heaven there is only one kind of all-consuming, unconditional love. The lessons about love we need to learn require physical form, and gaining our spiritual lessons on earth is the fastest way to learn.

From all this it seems that our spirits have the knowledge but, to truly understand, they need to *experience* in human form the emotions and feelings that can't be experienced in heaven. For example, our spirits may know that love is good and fear is bad, but only direct experience on earth can bring real understanding. In some ways, then, people who have crossed over to the other side are telling us that earth is a place we travel to in order to learn and grow, a bit like school.

It is especially hard to believe we actually choose our experiences on earth when life deals us a particularly harsh or painful blow. Immediately the 'why do bad things happen to good people?' question again comes to mind, and there seems no reason or sense in it, but I hope the third secret of heaven will show you that in spirit there may be perfect sense. We may not understand now why we are living through pain or heartache, but in spirit we will see that it was necessary for our soul's evolution. Heaven can disguise itself in the most unlikely and unwelcome ways, even through times of suffering, trauma and crisis. One metaphor I like to use, to help anyone who asks me understand, is to compare this life to the underside of an embroidery or tapestry. It's all messy ends and false starts but then, when you turn it over – in heaven – everything that didn't make sense or looked ugly before suddenly makes perfect and beautiful sense.

And just like any learning experience there will be challenges to overcome and things we both understand and don't understand, but when the lesson is over it is time to go back home, to our true home in heaven.

Fear vs. love

There are many lessons for us to live through and learn from in life but by far the greatest one of all is learning to choose love over fear. Each one of us will have countless moments in our lives when we are forced to make that choice and our courage is tested to the limit. This doesn't mean conquering fear, it means learning to cope with it not by avoiding it or denying it but by facing it with a heart full of love.

Many times in decades past when I read about horrible acts of cruelty and injustice I plunged into the depths of despair and wondered how to reconcile this with my belief in heaven, but the afterlife research I have done has given me some insight into why monstrous human beings who hurt other people exist. They help us understand what is good and right by contrasting it with the opposite. They show that it is not spirit that brings suffering into the world; it is humankind because we have the power of choice.

Choosing love and dismissing fear is choosing heaven in both this life and the next because hell is not a place but a choice we make when we don't choose love. Whenever I try to answer the 'why does evil exist?' question, I talk about evil being a creation of humankind and a victory of fear over love. Heaven does not bring evil into the world; we allow evil to enter it whenever our spirits make choices out of fear and not love. In short, suffering and evil exist because of souls making fear-based choices, and because they live in fear. The insecurity that accompanies this state of being often goes hand in hand with a powerful need to control others. This is why you find many fearful souls in the position of leadership. However, the more these souls encounter spirits filled with love, the weaker they become. Only love can expose and ultimately defeat evil; like a vampire when it encounters the light, it withers and dies.

Of course, it is not easy to offer forgiveness and love when you have been cruelly and unjustly treated, but it is the true path to heaven. The Dalai Lama once told the story of a monk who was sent to prison by the Chinese for two decades. Asked by the Dalai Lama if he ever knew fear during his period of captivity, he said he was afraid on only two occasions – when he almost lost compassion for his captors.

Forgiveness and offering compassion and love instead of anger and hate is perhaps the hardest choice in life we will ever have to make. It is a choice, a higher way, I know I have failed to make on many occasions. Deep down, though, I know that not forgiving is a very human reaction and the spiritual answer, the only way for me truly to find peace, is to make the spiritual choice and forgive. Learning to forgive is a work in progress, but I can say from experience that it's like anything: the more I practise forgiveness and compassion, the easier it gets.

Heaven is a choice on earth

Like many people, I've been guilty of looking for heaven outside myself: in looking good, in relationships, in my job, in earning money, in being praised and so on, but when I look outside of myself in this way I am choosing heaven in all the wrong places.

I think one of the reasons I fear looking within is that I might not like what I see. Perhaps I am not as spiritual, loving or as selfless as I think I should be? Perhaps I don't want to confront darker aspects of my personality? But in running away from the darkness within myself I am also running away from the inner light. And if I am brutally honest it is sometimes easier to hide behind my doubts, fears and uncertainties because they give me an excuse not to shine. It is almost as if I'm afraid of discovering my true power. In heaven there is no hiding from the light within us. There is no fear, no darkness – only the shining light of love.

The power of giving

Choosing love over fear is making a choice for life and defeating death. Death, remember, is not about endings but about the absence of love and compassion. If you choose love you will feel more alive than ever before because you will be in harmony with the compassionate spiritual energy that underpins the universe. If you choose fear you will stop the flow and will feel a sense of restlessness and confusion.

Forgiveness and looking within are powerful ways to align yourself with the unseen flow of things. Another potent method is to give unconditionally from the heart, because the more you give from your heart the more the universe will give back to you in return. A lot of us think that when we give to others this involves some kind of expense or loss to ourselves, but nothing could be further from the truth. If you give joyfully and unconditionally – because you want to help or create joy for the receiver, and not in a calculated way because you hope for a return or recognition – then you will be lighting the way and bringing heaven closer to earth with your actions.

Many people send me letters asking me why they don't feel happy or loved or supported and my response, as always, informed by my study of NDEs, is usually the same. I tell them that sometimes the universe works in mysterious ways but it is often the case that if you want to be loved you have to learn to love (and not need) others; if you want to be happy, help others be happy; if you want support or appreciation, support and appreciate others, and so on. Giving and receiving are the same as far as the spiritual flow of energy in the universe is concerned.

In a nutshell, the simplest way to invite what you want into your life is to give others what you want or to help them in some way. If you can't help them physically or emotionally you can send them silent healing thoughts or prayers instead. The more you choose to give to others, the more you will receive. The more you choose to bring love, joy, support, peace and beauty into the lives of others, the more you attract all these heavenly gifts into your life. So what's stopping you? From this moment on, give everyone you meet a gift – even if that is just the gift of a smile or your time or a silent prayer. Heaven will be taking note.

And when things aren't going your way, don't use this as an excuse not to give; turn the situation around. Learn from your disappointment or mistake and try to educate others going through the same situation. If there is nothing you feel you can learn or teach others from a negative experience, take the higher spiritual road and rise above it. Sometimes horrible things happen for reasons our human selves cannot understand. Karma is a word that is often used, and if you believe in reincarnation you will perhaps believe we are taught lessons from our previous lives. Some, but certainly not all, NDE stories do seem to provide evidence for reincarnation, so perhaps there truly are karmic reasons for experiences in our lives. Whether or not that is the case, as some NDE stories do not include it, one message comes across loud and clear: we are spiritual beings having a human experience, not the other way around, and what happens to us on earth is a result of the spiritual choices we make or don't make.

Choices, choices, choices

The highest spiritual values can come from the study of death.

Elizabeth Kübler-Ross

Every instant of our lives we are making conscious and unconscious choices and what happens to you in this life and the next is the result of these choices. I hope heavenly secret number three has encouraged you to take a moment to reflect on the choices you are making right now – in this instant. A lot of the time we make choices without even taking time to think because it's something we have always done or because other people expect it of us, but I hope from now on you will take time to become fully aware of the choices you are making. Ask yourself if this is what your heart wants, and if it will make you and others happy. If you aren't sure, take some time out before rushing in. And if you still aren't sure, ask your heart – it will always know the right answer and fill you with feelings of comfort and happiness when you make that right decision.

I'll end this section with yet another profound truth that NDE stories teach us: your future life on earth and in heaven is determined by the choices you make every moment of your life, starting right here, right now.

4. POSSIBILITY

The fourth Secret of Heaven is the exciting power of **possibility**.

> *Not only are we in the Universe, the Universe is in us. I don't know of any deeper spiritual feeling than what that brings upon me.*
>
> Neil Tyson

All the secrets of heaven revealed through NDEs are based on the truth that we are eternal spiritual beings. Our consciousness is our true spirit or self, the part of us that never dies and is pure joy, love, creativity and bliss. It is also the part of us that is infinite possibility.

Understanding that the real you is spirit is an incredibly liberating, intoxicating concept, as you realise that you don't need to seek approval from others any more, and that happiness can never be achieved by material things or controlling circumstances or people or things. None of these things can truly satisfy your spirit. True happiness can only ever be found within you because you understand your spiritual nature. You know that everyone you encounter is part of the same energy – just in a different body. We are all infinite possibility and potential, interconnected in spirit.

Guiding Lights

In the light I felt capable of everything, linked to everything. There was no past or future, just the present. Everything was one. I also felt that every possibility was happening. I saw this in action. I saw myself in my car at a junction. I turned left and right and straight ahead at the same time. Sounds trippy, doesn't it, but in my NDE it made perfect sense. Everything connects to everything. I carried this insight back with me into my life and never dismiss anything as random or coincidence again because it isn't. Steve

I saw everyone and everything as energy and our energy level created our world. If love was in our energy we would attract opportunities to express that love, but if hate or anger was in our energy we would attract obstacles. We aren't physical in the way we think we are – I think the physical is how our energy expresses itself. We can change our physical reality by changing our energy vibration. Back on earth I have become very tuned into my energy levels as a result, and I feel they are at their most potent when I live in the moment with joy and love. I know that living in this way will change my future. This sounds so simple but when I was experiencing the understanding of it during my NDE I knew it was infinitely profound. Michael

Synchronicity

And nothing illustrates the divine interconnectedness of everything and the sense of possibility this uncovers better than coincidences or, to use the spiritual term for coincidence, synchronicity. I strongly believe that synchronicity is the language that heaven speaks on earth, and if more of us recognised the magic of synchronicity in our lives we would hear heaven calling our name.

Coincidences appear like chance events but, to those who experience them, they can often feel like part of a carefully orchestrated plan for their lives. Let's get something clear right from the start: heaven will not run your life or intrude on your free will. It will not interfere or issue commands but it will try to open your mind and heart instead and gently guide you onto a path that will lead to happiness and hope. And one of heaven's favourite ways to encourage and guide us along is through synchronicity.

Have you ever been in a situation when you are thinking about someone and then they call or send an email? Or perhaps you've gone on holiday and met someone you went to school with? Or maybe a song popped into your head and then, minutes later, you hear it playing on the radio? Most of the time we forget about these kinds of coincidences, but coincidences are the way heaven tries to talk to us. Sometimes paying attention to and opening your mind to a coincidence, even if it's a subtle one, can have a powerful, life-changing effect. And every now and again, it can have a truly universal effect. You're probably familiar with the story of Isaac Newton, the seventeenth-century scientist who formulated the laws of gravity, but it is such a beautiful example of synchronicity at work that I'd like you to bear with me and read about it one more time.

In junior school you may have heard how Newton made his great discovery not in a science lab but in the garden of his mother's home while on holiday. He went into the garden, meditating on the 'why' questions of nature, and as he sat there an apple fell from a nearby tree. Most people wouldn't have given it a second thought, but for Newton's questioning mind it was a moment of truth. He instantly understood that the law of the universe is attraction of mass to mass. This isn't confined to earth alone but is a principle that applies from planet to planet, star to star. It is this mutual attraction – the law of gravity – that keeps everything in the universe in its place. Some conclude that Newton's theory suggests there is no higher power, but in my opinion the event was more than just coincidence. A higher force was involved. Heaven wanted to open Newton's brilliant mind to how beautiful and ordered the world is – and to do this an apple was chosen – perhaps to counteract the disorder and sin that had marked the world when an earlier apple was plucked from a tree.

Certainly in my many years of collecting angel stories I have often marvelled at how apparently trivial events, like an apple falling from a tree or a lost object being unexpectedly found, can have an incredible effect. As Barbara explains in her story over the page, the coincidences obviously can't match the universal effect of Newton's story, but from a personal point of view the impact was profound.

Lost and Found

Fred and I were sweethearts at school and, as soon as we left school we got engaged. We wanted to get married as soon as possible but postponed the wedding because of the war. The next five years were tough – very tough indeed – and my heart fluttered every time the doorbell rang or the mail arrived. We wrote to each other as much as we could, and I tried to get on with my life, but it was torture being apart. I still have every one of Ian's letters and he kept every one of mine. To take his mind off things I talked in my letters to him a lot about our wedding and he talked a lot about the ring he wanted to buy me. He told me he wanted me to have the most beautiful wedding band ever and he wanted the ring to be engraved.

So many of my friends lost their sweethearts when they were posted overseas but, by the mercy of God, Ian came back safely to me. We didn't get married straight away, as we needed to save some money, but after a few years the day I had been waiting so long for arrived. It was every bit as beautiful as I had wished and the wedding ring Ian gave me was incredible. I still to this day have no idea how he afforded it. It was beautifully designed and at least half an inch wide and engraved on it were the words, 'Our love is true and for ever', with our wedding date: 9/6/50.

We went to Scotland for three weeks for our honeymoon and every second was magic. On the last evening we went out for one more romantic meal by the lakeside. Feeling a little stuffed we decided to walk along the lake and, it being our honeymoon, we decided to have a cuddle on the shore. Eventually, we headed back to the hotel and I started to get ready for bed. It was then that I realised my wedding ring was gone. Frantically we searched everywhere in the hotel room. We phoned the restaurant the next morning and retraced our steps along the lake, but there was no sign of the ring. You can imagine how upset I was, especially as Ian had talked about the ring so much and saved up to buy it.

We did all we could but, eventually, we had to admit defeat – the ring was gone. On the way back home in the coach I found it hard to fight back the tears. Ian comforted me as best he could and told me that I didn't need a ring to know how much he loved me. Rings were easy to buy but our love and companionship wasn't.

A few months later, Ian bought me an equally gorgeous ring, and although I was very happy with it I never told him that I always yearned for the first one.

Twenty years and three kids later, I was as much in love with Ian as I had ever been. Life was good and the children a constant source of delight, but my happiness was to be shattered when, on the 1st June 1972, he was killed in a car accident. I was told that he had died instantly and that he didn't suffer but my pain was unbearable. Almost all my life Ian had been in my thoughts and in my heart and I had no idea how I would cope without him. Of course, I had to be strong with the kids, but when I was alone the tears never stopped flowing. I begged him to send me a sign that he was still with me.

I decided to scatter Ian's ashes in Scotland, as we had both been so happy there on our honeymoon. When we arrived, Ian's sister had organised a light fish supper for us at a restaurant with a fine reputation that had recently opened. I found it hard to eat but I forced a morsel or two into my mouth. Perhaps I didn't chew my food properly before swallowing, or perhaps my throat was really dry because of all the crying, but I started to choke on something, probably a fish bone. I couldn't breathe but mercifully the feeling passed and I was able to swallow. By then the manager had rushed to my side ready to administer first aid and he was mighty relieved to see that I was OK. I was relieved too, as nearly choking to death reminded me how much I had to live for – my grandchildren and my children needed me. I was also relieved because my eyes were streaming not with tears as they had been for the last week but as a reaction to the choking.

With the incident over, a concerned-looking waitress about the same age as me asked me if I was OK. I nodded and said that it was more the shock and the embarrassment now. She smiled at me and told me that a few years back her husband had nearly choked on an earring that had somehow made its way into a fish's stomach. It had been a really scary couple of minutes. 'Fish end up eating the strangest things,' she went on to say. 'I've even heard stories of people choking on buttons and rings found in fish's stomachs.' As soon as she mentioned rings I thought about my long-lost wedding ring and wondered out loud if some fish had eaten it all those years ago.

You could have knocked me over with a feather when I heard the waitress tell me that about twenty years ago she had found a wedding ring when she was out walking her dog along the lakeside one morning. She saw her dog scratching in the sand and then put something in his mouth. She couldn't believe her eyes when he spat out a gold wedding ring. Shakily, I asked her if the ring was engraved with the words 'our love is true and for ever', and she nodded. I told her that the wedding ring was mine and I'd lost it on my honeymoon.

The waitress was only too happy to return the ring to me. She had been tempted to sell it on many occasion but for some reason she couldn't explain she had decided to keep it all these years. She told me she had placed an advertisement in the local newspaper but everyone who tried to claim it hadn't guessed the right words engraved on it so she knew they were frauds.

Later that night I stood by the very lakeside where I had lost my ring all those years ago but this time it had found its way back to its true owner and was glittering on my hand in the moonlight. You can call it a series of strange coincidences if you like, but for me it is proof that my beloved Ian is watching over me.

Unsurprisingly Barbara has never let her lost and found ring out of her sight since. It is a constant reminder that in this life and the next the love between her and Ian is true and for ever. It is very hard to read a story like this and not to think that heaven played a hand.

And, as if to underline this point, meaningful coincidences tend to increase in people's lives after a NDE. Here's what Becky wrote and told me.

Serendipity

I enjoyed your chapter on coincidences very much because since I 'died' I now notice them everywhere. When I had my NDE there was this blinding sense of perfect connection and everything made sense and meaning because everything was interrelated. It was like taking a swim in a sea of comforting serendipity, if that doesn't sound too odd. I haven't been able to carry that feeling of perfect and total bliss and understanding back into my life but I know where to look for it first. I look for it in coincidences. Heaven taught me that there are no coincidences. That is simply our word for things that our physical minds can't explain from a rational perspective. I saw in my NDE that everything is crafted, designed – even mistakes or accidents.

Let me explain: when an accident happens it is because one person or thing is creating in one place and another person or thing is creating in another and they have an interaction that is unexpected. So an accident happens, but most of the time coincidence is heaven talking to us and creating something.

This isn't to say that I think everything that happens to me is meaningful. Sometimes a bus going past is just a bus going past, nothing more and nothing less, but what I am trying to express here is that my NDE gave me a total sense of the oneness, the interconnection of all things and that coincidences are serendipity.

In her book, *Dying to Be Me*, Anita Moorjani also talked about a heightened awareness of coincidences following her NDE, which taught her that, '*Nothing that happens on earth exists on its own – everything is in the context of the universe.*'

Subtle patterns

Of course, you could write all this off as chance, but then again, what is chance? Is anything in this life truly random?

You may have noticed that all the stories in this book so far have a common theme and that is clarity coming out of confusion, order coming out of chaos, pain emerging from hope and certainty coming when there is doubt. Many of us feel confused and uncertain, and it's all too easy to believe that everything that happens to us is chaotic and random.

Atheists present Chaos Theory as the answer to anyone who believes their life is something more than a random event, but in the last few decades scientists have discovered a new meaning to Chaos Theory which suggests there are subtle patterns to chaos. Take the miracle of DNA, for instance, or the human circulatory system or the intricate design of a snowflake. There is nothing random here, just a perfect design in which everything has a place, function and purpose. To illustrate the point further you need only to look at the natural world, where patterns and an unexplained intelligence can often be seen. Take salmon, for example – just how do they find their way to their spawning grounds every year?

Even scientists are slowly beginning to accept there may be an underlying order to everything. I'm sure you have all heard of the butterfly effect theory, where a single occurrence, no matter how small, can change the course of our lives forever. The example often given is that the flap of a butterfly's wings changes the air around it to create a tiny air current, which set off corresponding changes in the environment until a tornado breaks out two continents away.

From a spiritual perspective the butterfly effect points to the universal truth that we are all one in spirit. It could also signal the importance of and interconnection between our thoughts, words and actions. Although scientific theory can't yet bring itself to acknowledge a spiritual power creating this world, theories like this, and quantum studies, suggest that scientists have started to break away from their past methods of presenting scientific theories and are slowly beginning to recognise what NDEs make abundantly clear: the interconnectedness of the universe.

Therefore, Secret of Heaven Number Four is about becoming aware of yourself as infinite possibility, interconnected with everything and everyone in spirit. In NDE accounts this is how heaven is felt and experienced, and bringing this understanding into our earthly lives draws the creative energy and endless possibilities of the universe towards you. Seeing yourself in others creates a bond of love and understanding and opens the door to infinite potential. Recognising the hand of heaven in everything you say and do, however trivial, lets magic into your life. Not only do you start to attract what is positive and beautiful, you also become more effortlessly creative and inspired. Other people are instinctively drawn to your self-awareness and inner joy and the feelings of love, hope and possibility you inspire in them. You become an inspiration, a celestial and serene light to guide, enlighten and empower others to discover who they really are.

In other words, the universe is you and you are the universe. You are a universe of infinite magic, possibility and unlimited potential.

5. CALM

The fifth Secret of Heaven is the serene beauty of inner **calm**.

Calmness is the cradle of power.

Josiah Gilbert Holland

Whenever I read NDE stories I notice that something remarkable happens, starting from the inside out. Whatever I'm doing and whatever mood I'm in a profound feeling of calm and stillness comes over me. This even happens when I read stories outside the relative quiet of my office. Once I was on the Tube and missed my stop because I was reflecting so deeply about what I had just read and, when I eventually realised my mistake, I didn't get stressed or angry with myself – quite the opposite. I was pleased, as it meant a chance to re-read the story on the way back. I'd be surprised if reading this next story doesn't have a calming effect on you.

Heart Stopping

My heart stopped three times, I later learned from the doctors. Here's what happened to me. I floated out of my body and turned around to see it. It felt like I was in space. I could see all the machines and the drip and the doctors trying to restart my heart. It was pretty dramatic stuff. I saw my husband and my mother waiting anxiously outside the room. I felt for them and sent healing love because they looked stressed, but I felt so peaceful, warm and light. I was bathed in such calm. The peace was overwhelming.

Then I felt a very powerful force pulling me away from the chaos below towards a serene and beautiful place or higher realm. I travelled very slowly through a tunnel but the tunnel wasn't dark or scary; it was tranquil and filled with rainbow colours and shining stars. I knew I was heading towards a bright light and, the closer I got, the deeper I fell into a trance of peace, stillness and whiteness. I wanted to walk into the whiteness, lose myself in it, as it was so beautiful and happy. I can't say what was there because there was nothing to look at as such, just a tremendous feeling of bliss. I felt OK, as if I was at home. I was relaxed – completely and utterly relaxed.

I felt at one with the power of the universe and part of something bigger and yet I was also the whole of it. It was hugely empowering but also profoundly calming.

I can't relinquish the calming feeling my voyage to heaven gave me. I have seen pure heart-stopping beauty and it has totally refreshed me and given me stillness, powerful stillness. Whereas before I was quite an obsessive and anxious person

– always needing to be in control – now I am the very model of serenity and calm. Why wouldn't I be? I've truly seen the profound stillness of heaven. Paul

Accounts like this focus our minds and hearts on the importance of inner calm to form a deep connection with spirit on earth. In heaven there is no turmoil, just beautiful serenity, and if we want to catch a glimpse of heaven on earth one of the most effective ways is to find stillness within.

Moments of silence

Let peace be your middle name.

Ntathu Allen

Secret Number Five is all about becoming aware of yourself as a spiritual being in moments of silence, contemplation or meditation – or, if meditation is not for you, walking in nature or doing things you love are other ways to get in touch with your true self and your interconnection with all that is. In those reflective moments of stillness and non-judgement, you become a human *being* and not a human *doing*, and these moments can be a source of unbounded creativity. You get in touch with the deepest essence of who you really are, and this essence, as we saw in Secret Number Four, is pure magic. The sky really is the limit.

Meditation

Meditation is a practice that almost every spiritual teacher recommends, but if you've read any of my books previously you'll know that meditation is something I have tried and failed at many times. Even during the course of writing this book I tried yet again, with a course of tapes that utilise the power of sacred sound developed by Dr Karen Newell and Dr Eben Alexander (www.sacredacoustics.com). I kept a journal of my progress and here is a snapshot:

Just say OM

The first challenge was finding the time and peace and quiet. Not easy if you are busy or live in a noisy household. The second challenge was trying not to giggle at myself when I switched the tape on and heard the OM-like sounds. The third challenge was not falling asleep. The fourth challenge was not thinking about all the things I should be doing but aren't doing because I'm lying down and trying to meditate.

I'm a natural-born fidget and my mind is always racing with ideas, so it wasn't easy to just relax. However – and this is exciting – after a while the sacred tones really started to absorb me. I found myself drawn into a sound world somehow like a vortex. I was grateful to Karen's calming voice offering gentle suggestions along the way, as that gave me a point of focus. In time, though, I wasn't visualising anything. It was all about the sound. I felt in one moment that I had stepped inside the sound, if that doesn't sound too strange.

I think I lost time once (which probably means I fell asleep) and, towards the end, instead of images, feelings and thoughts, there was total nothingness – like a dark but blank canvas. This was initially a bit frightening but also liberating. I was there but I wasn't there. I was outside myself. As the tape came to an end, I felt a little reluctant to open my eyes and go back to reality. When I did open my eyes, instead of feeling groggy as I'd expected, I was wide-awake. Was that because I'd had a power nap, or was it because I had entered into another realm of consciousness? I really don't know but I look forward to continuing my meditation journey and seeing if any answers, insights and images emerge.

My second meditation attempt was very different, perhaps because I knew what to expect, so I didn't get the giggles as much this time when I started chanting OM. There is something very calming and inspiring about OM and I've asked sacred acoustics creator Karen Newell to explain its history and why it is so soothing. This is what she said:

> OM is a mantra best known in the Hindu tradition as the primordial sound in the universe. We found that by vocalizing 'OM' at the start of listening to the tones, it enhanced our experience. This came about from personal experimentation, not from a particular spiritual tradition. Most of our recordings begin with these frequencies. I liken it to an activation of the energy body. By creating the vibration in one's body, these vibrations then intermingle with the tones, allowing the tones to carry you on the journey. We have created tones with a base of harmonic carrier frequencies.

So, back to my meditation. As I listened to the tape, something very surprising happened. For no reason at all I felt elated, just happy to be alive and in the moment. That was a real gift. Going deeper into the meditation things felt darker and it was hard to stop my mind thinking of all the things I should be doing instead of meditating, but I think I achieved stillness for a while. The dark nothingness that replaced my racing thoughts felt strange, as it did the day before, like I was falling from a great height, but there was no fear of the fall, just acceptance, which has to be progress, right? I truly hope in time that the dark nothingness will be the place I get flashes of insight and inspiration. Or perhaps nothingness is what I need and it's the place where seeds of inspiration grow.

I also asked Karen why I sometimes feel tearful while meditating. She explained:

> Listening to the tones can activate emotions stored in the energy field. Tears reflect much more than sadness, they are an indicator of emotional release. There is no need to analyse or know 'why' – simply allow the release. Some experience this very strongly. It has been shown to allow for deeper, more meaningful experience in later listening sessions.

Only time will tell, but I will keep working on this. And I have kept using the tapes, as they are beautiful and calming, but I am probably one of those people who prefers to find their own path to meditation – or, as I prefer to think of it, their time of inner calm, stillness and quiet.

Going within

Meditation can certainly be a wonderful tool for achieving clarity of vision and a peaceful state of mind, but there is a warning attached: meditation may not work for everyone. As you saw before, it doesn't typically work for me, as I often fall asleep whenever I make a concerted effort to try it. Perhaps one of the reasons I struggle with it is that I am one of those people who always likes to be doing. I'm not very good at just being and meditation is all about being. It is all about being yourself; just you in the moment.

There are tools and techniques that can help you get into a meditative state, but in some ways these tools and techniques fall short because, in its purest form, meditation is something you cannot actually *do*. It just happens. And it can happen at any time, not necessarily when you are kneeling on a yoga mat and doing deep-breathing exercises. I have had profound moments of clarity at the most unexpected times, usually when I'm totally absorbed in an activity, day-dreaming, feeling a sense of wonder or my heart is bursting with joy. And that is probably why I find meditation as a practice difficult. I'm straining to make something happen and thinking if I learn certain techniques I will get there, but to risk repeating myself meditation is about being not doing. So, although meditation works wonders for some people, and I recommend you try it, until I fully master the technique myself I'm going to give you a new perspective – a perspective that works for me. Here goes:

The meditative state is your natural state. It can't be created, learned or possessed; it just has to be noticed. It is already there for you and always has been. It is your being. It is you – your spirit – and your task is to reconnect with it. A lot of people confuse meditation with contemplation or mind control, but meditation is not about thought at all. It is about the lack of thought. That's why meditation techniques – such as imagining thoughts turning into butterflies – aren't always effective because these techniques just put more thoughts into your head. What you need to do is stop thinking and trying altogether. You must do, think and feel nothing. Just be.

Returning to just being is a challenge because so many of us lead busy and stressful lives and are used to *doing*, but if you are able to regularly set aside time to come back to yourself in this way, you will experience remarkable inner clarity and vision. And this inner clarity could transform your life completely as you start to notice everything you say and do from the inside out. You become consciously aware of the energy within you. All your thoughts and feelings just vanish so that what is left is just the silence of you.

Watching yourself from the inside out feels surreal at first but I urge you to give it a try. Spend a few minutes noticing every movement, action, word, feeling and thought you have from within. Pay conscious attention to everything you do. After a while something amazing will happen. You will notice that the real you is actually separate from all these things. When you notice this separation, you will gradually begin to distance yourself from your thoughts, feelings and actions. You will start to identify with your inner glow because you know it is truly you.

Then something even more remarkable will happen – someone else, typically someone sensitive, will begin to notice your inner glow. The light inside you will reach them. There may be no words or physical contact but they feel touched by you in some inexplicable way. There is a spiritual connection between you that you cannot explain and, in time, that connection will extend to another person and another and another and so on. Then it will extend to animals and the natural world and, from there, to the universe and beyond. What you will then experience is a mystical connection between all people and things – past, present and future, living and in spirit. There are many ways to describe this sensational experience but I call it heaven.

Don't try

To sum up: the meditative, receptive, mystical state may only be fully realised in the afterlife, but it is possible to catch glimpses of it on earth in moments of inner calm and stillness. Each one of us must find our own way to inner peace. Meditation may or may not work for you but, whatever method you employ, perhaps the most important thing to remember is not to force things or try too hard. Straining just creates stress and tension and shuts your mind to the possibility of heaven in the process.

Bear in mind that the attitude that will most nourish your connection to heaven is respect – for yourself, for others, for nature, for life itself – both here and on the other side. Wherever there is respect, feelings of tenderness, awe and wonder are never far behind, creating fertile ground for spiritual growth. And along with a respectful attitude, to achieve a state of inner calm you also need to discover for yourself the truth of the words, 'less is more' and the power of acceptance.

If you look at the world of nature, the grass does not try to grow and the sun does not try to shine and so on. It all just happens naturally. NDE stories show us that heaven is 'calm effortlessness' because everything there is connected by the energy of love. When your life on earth is based around love there is never any shortage of energy to manifest materially in your life in terms of happiness and perhaps even wealth and success. But if your life is centred around power, the desire for money and so on, energy is drained and the result is unhappiness and feelings of emptiness, regardless of your life circumstances. If everything in your life is about you and your need for approval, status or control, then this is the greatest energy drain of all.

Acceptance is simply living in the moment and knowing that everything is as it should be. You acknowledge things as they are and understand that if you feel angry or hurt by anyone or anything, it is not the person or situation that's causing you distress but your feelings about that person or situation. With this realisation you can empower yourself to make positive changes because you will be taking responsibility for your life and not seeking to blame outside forces. You will also have the insight to know that every problem, challenge or obstacle in your life is an opportunity to grow and learn spiritually. This takes us back to Secret of Heaven Number Three: Choice – where you learned from NDEs that this life is very much like school or university.

With this great understanding you will be able to remain calm and accepting in the present moment, even when faced with hurtful people or situations, because you will know that each moment is as it should be, and that each moment disguises a powerful lesson or teacher. You will also no longer have any need to try to control, blame or convince others of your viewpoint, or even to hold a fixed point of view, because you will be open to all possibilities and perspectives. There will be no need for you to react because you will have become one with spirit and can rise above whatever life throws at you.

Living in the present, knowing this moment is what it should be, will bring you the freedom, joy and beauty of inner calm. You will see problems as opportunities and know that just being you is enough to attract all you need to make your dreams come true.

The power of the present moment

We've now reached the mid-way mark with the Secrets of Heaven revealed through NDE accounts, and I'm fully aware that a lot of what has been revealed may be pretty hard to get your head around. It's a subject that's far easier talked about than lived and experienced.

Let's have a brief recap: Secret One taught the simple but profound truth that we are spiritual beings having a human experience and not vice versa; Secret Two was all about the power of prayer and the intention to attract what you desire into your life; Secret Three stressed the importance of free will and choice and the power generated when you choose love over fear; Secret Four put forward the notion that we are all interconnected and nothing on this earth is random, and Secret Five revealed the profound spiritual significance of inner calm.

The first four secrets are enlightening and deeply thought-provoking. Perhaps in the days, weeks and months ahead, some of their insights will trickle into your awareness and, by so doing, transform your life by letting in glimpses of heaven. Secret Five is slightly different, though, as it's a more practical, 'apply right here right now' revelation because it requires you to become aware of the true power and potential of the present moment.

Let's face it, the only thing that exists is right now. The past is history and tomorrow is potential but right now exists. It's a precious gift and that's why it is called the present. Yesterday and tomorrow are memories and expectations. Today is where the power to change your life lies. If you don't like what is going on for you today, use the power of the present moment to change your thoughts and actions into loving and kind ones, so that you start to attract what is good and joyful.

Know how

The Power of Now concept is far easier to understand than to actually apply, but I can suggest a few techniques that may help. The reason your mind has trouble living in the present moment and finding inner calm is simply because it doesn't know how. It is not used to focusing on the here and now. It needs retraining.

Begin to sharpen your awareness by asking yourself if, in the present moment, you are waiting for something to happen. Are you waiting for the right person or the right opportunity or more money or a flash of inspiration? If you answer yes to any of this, than you are not living in the present moment. Of course, it's impossible to live in the Now 24/7 – that heightened state of awareness can only happen in the afterlife – but you can start by putting yourself there for a few minutes each day.

The next time you walk anywhere pay attention to what is happening around you. Listen to the sounds, observe everything and everyone, and shut off thoughts about anything that isn't what you can hear, see, smell or touch right now. Focus your attention only on what is happening right now. Like anything, the more you practise the better you will get, and the easier it will be for you to focus your mind and utilise the power and potential of Now.

You will probably notice that when you do things you love, or are with people you love – in other words when your heart is involved – it's so much easier to live in the Now. Whenever fear is involved, the present slips away, because fear always takes us away from the Now into anxiety about the future or regret about the past. So let love be your guide, not fear. If you have a passion for music, then sing or play an instrument or listen to the music you adore. If you have a passion for cooking or painting or sports, lose yourself in the art or craft. It's the same whenever something makes you laugh or you have fun. The reason these things are so liberating is because, for those few moments of laughter, you are fully present and fully engaged in the Now. You lose track of time and that is like heaven because, if you remember, near-death-experiencers always say that in heaven there is no longer an awareness of time.

Do what you love and you will naturally live in the present more often and start attracting positive people and situations into your life. You will also be more likely to achieve perhaps the deepest state of inner calm and transcendence that is possible to achieve on earth – the so-called peak experience.

Waking up to heaven

From time to time we all experience a higher state of consciousness, when a deep and profound inner peace settles upon us and, for a while, the world is a place of magic and beauty where everything pulsates with a life force. We feel we are at one with all things, that the world is a loving place, and we may even become aware of a higher force than ourselves encompassing everyone and everything.

During these incredible moments we see the world from a higher perspective. It is as if we glimpse the world as it truly is and a blindfold has been removed. I think every new mother will have glimpsed this awareness in a quiet moment alone with her newborn baby. Others may experience it when they fall in love or when the beauty of the natural world takes their breath away. The trigger may be meditation, art, music or yoga or during sex or sport or exercise. It may occur after bouts of depression when suddenly hope appears again. Or there may be no trigger other than a moment of profound spiritual awareness.

Science and psychology have attempted to explain away these feelings as caused by stress or endorphins or even brain malfunction. The suggestion is that spiritual feelings which offer glimpses of another reality are illusions or pleasant deviations from normal brain and psychological function, but NDE accounts teach us that the so-called peak experience is a higher state of consciousness and is what we are likely to experience in heaven. Therefore, our ordinary consciousness or perception of reality is the illusion here; peak experience is our highest level of awareness because heaven is our real home.

It is often said that children are closer to heaven and this may be because children live constantly in a hightened state of awareness. The world around them is a magical pace, and they feel awe and see magic in things adults find routine. A child's ego and accompanying fears and doubts are not yet fully developed and, because of this, they are tuned into the invisible world of spirit. It is sad that as adults we lose this magical and vibrant connection. During peak experiences, however, when we discover within ourselves all the beauty, peace and magic we need, we wake up and, for a few remarkable moments, actually see, feel and experience what life is truly like in heaven.

6. INTUITION

The sixth Secret of Heaven revealed by NDE accounts is the divine power of **intuition**.

> *The intuitive mind is a sacred gift and the rational mind is a faithful servant. We have created a society that honours the servant but has forgotten the gift.*
>
> Einstein

NDE stories, like the following, seem to show that in heaven our intuitive powers are so fully developed that telepathy is the only form of communication.

No Need for Words

I was met by a being of light. It was not of human form and there were no words. We communicated mind to mind, like some form of spiritual telepathy. John

> The higher up I floated the brighter the light became. An angel appeared and we drifted towards the light. We communicated without words and through our thoughts. It was instant. I was told I was being guided back home. Lucy

> I saw my grandfather in heaven. He spoke to me. His lips did not move but I understood everything he said. I spoke to him too and my lips did not move. Nadia

> As I re-entered my body I felt myself drawn to another room in the hospital. Lying on the bed was a man and I knew he was dying. He was in a coma. I spoke to him without words and he spoke to me. He asked me to tell his wife and family how much he loved them and that he was sorry he had gone to the shops. After I had recovered I tried to find the room I had visited but it was empty. I asked the nurses and they said, yes, a man had died on the day of my operation. I asked why he was in a coma and they said he had been involved in a car crash at a busy junction. I know that junction and it is close to some shops. I have often thought of trying to get in touch with his family to tell them but the hospital wouldn't give me any details. So instead I try to send them a message with my thoughts. I think they can hear me – I believe completely in the power of telepathy after my NDE. Arthur

In much the same way as Secret Number Five reveals to us through peak experiences a glimpse of what it feels like to be in heaven, Secret Number Six reveals how communication and interaction happens in heaven. There is an absolute understanding of everyone and everything, and we instantly know the answer to any question we may have had in our lives. Communication with other spirits occurs through telepathy or reading thoughts. There is no need for words.

Intuition on earth

We have all experienced times when we knew with certainty that something was happening or was going to happen. When that occurs, there is no doubt; just an absolute knowing, which usually proves to be accurate. Similarly, there will have been times when you understood absolutely what someone was thinking without them uttering a word. Sixth sense, psychic power, clairvoyance or telepathy are the terms most often used to describe this super sense – the cumulative power of all the senses – but perhaps the simplest way to describe it is intuition.

We all have intuition but most of us aren't aware of it, or use it only occasionally. Intuition isn't something some people have but others lack; some people are simply more aware of their abilities, or more naturally sensitive than others. Rest assured that the potential is there within you; it is simply a forgotten art that needs to be rediscovered and developed.

If you have ever experienced any of the following, or just felt that you might have, this is your intuition calling you direct from heaven:

- *Sometimes you dream about something or get a hunch or gut feeling and it comes true and turns out to be right*
- *Sometimes you just know what someone else is thinking*
- *Perhaps you thought about someone and then they called or texted*
- *When you walk into a room or space you sense the atmosphere or know when someone is angry, upset or excited before they speak to you*
- *You sometimes have a sudden feeling that you should or should not go somewhere and then found out later that you should have listened to that feeling*

In heaven the intuitive power that we glimpse sporadically on earth is fully developed. There is complete and total understanding of everyone and everything, as you step into an existence of limitless potential. You don't have to wait until you cross over to the other side, though, to access the astonishing power of your intuition. As mentioned above, we are all born with intuitive power – we just fail to recognise or use it, but it is possible to rediscover, train and develop it every day, much as you would build up your physical fitness. In many ways, developing your intuition is a journey of spiritual discovery – rediscovering your inborn psychic powers and who you really are and where you are going.

So where do you start?

You start by crossing a very special line – the line between your physical self and your spiritual self, or the world beyond your five senses. The non-psychic side of your life is informed by your five senses. Your ears, ears, nose, mouth and skin constantly provide you with information, so the first step is to become more aware of your senses – the sights, sounds, smells and feel of things around you. Only when you become more aware of the physical can you start to tell when you are getting information without using your five senses.

So what is on the psychic side? The answer is fairly simple: your thoughts and becoming aware of a world inside your head that is different from the physical world is where you begin. This is the world where your psychic power will reveal itself. Feeling, hearing and seeing your thoughts is the beginning of intuitive development. Intuition is knowing something without being aware that you know it.

For me the terms intuition and psychic power are interchangeable because they are both a bridge between the physical and spiritual part of our nature. Simply put, intuition is a piece of heaven in our DNA that can see the bigger picture of our lives and help us listen to our inner wisdom.

Talking to heaven

Feelings of awe, respect and wonder will encourage the development of your intuitive or psychic powers. Just as certain foods nourish you better than others, veneration and respect, when combined with honest intention, is the perfect diet for stimulating spiritual growth. Self-interest, competitiveness, the desire to control are like junk food and will have the opposite effect.

Holding the idea of respect and awe in your head and heart, as you work through the suggestions below, will give your intuition a powerful boost. If you are having trouble with this, think back to your childhood and what inspired awe and wonder in you then. If that doesn't enlighten you, think of something sensationally beautiful and awe-inspiring in nature, like a stunning rainbow or a sunset.

Recognise it: Just recognising that intuition is a legitimate channel through which you can receive divine guidance. Committing to developing it will start the process. Pay attention to the thoughts that enter your mind and the feelings in your heart. Don't dismiss them as foolish or not relevant or something that may be obvious to others. In the great majority of cases, what is obvious to you is not obvious to everyone else.

Record it: If your mobile has a record option, get into the habit of recording the random thoughts that come to you. If you don't want to use a mobile, carry a simple notepad with you – it will serve the same purpose. Keeping a record of your insights like this will give your thoughts a chance to express themselves instead of being stifled or dismissed. It will also, in time, give you an opportunity to assess how accurate they were. For example, did your feelings of unease about someone you were introduced to prove to be true?

Ask questions. Open a Word document or get a piece of paper and a pen and ask a question. Type, or write, whatever comes into your mind, however nonsensical. It doesn't matter if what you write down reads crazy. No one is going to read it but you. Don't think about what you are writing – just write automatically.

Get fresh air. Divine guidance can come through a quiet and calm mind more easily than a distracted one. Over the years one of the best ways I've found to clear my mind is by going for a walk, preferably in the countryside, but if that isn't possible a walk around the block will do the trick. I mentioned previously how I often find it hard to meditate. Instead of relaxing and quieting my mind, meditation either makes me feel tense because I can't master the techniques, or sleepy because closing my eyes is the cue for my body to fall asleep. Walking briskly, on the other hand, and getting fresh air, not only calms me and gives me much-needed time out, it also helps sharpen my mind, so I can hear my thoughts and be more receptive to and aware of heavenly communication.

Stare at a plant: Observe a young plant closely. Notice everything about it – its colour, shape and texture. Now let this thought fill your mind: one day this plant will become a bigger plant. Now picture in your mind this bigger plant – see in your mind what it will one day become. This exercise will take time but keep working at it because you will start to notice results, and when that happens your intuitive understanding of living things as bursting with potential will evolve.

Suspend your disbelief: This is perhaps the most challenging but also the most enlightening method to increase your intuitive awareness – and the best way to seek inspiration for this guideline is to see the world again through the eyes of a child. Read on for further explanation:

Nurture your inner child

I'd like to begin here by sharing this story about a little girl called Anna, sent in to me by her mother, Sasha.

Night-night

About a week ago I was getting my four-year-old daughter, Anna, ready for bed. I read her a story and gave her a cuddle and she seemed to settle down nicely. This was something of a miracle in itself because, for the last few months, she had really struggled to fall asleep and there had been quite a few tears and tantrums. I was at breaking-point really. I really need my sleep and when Anna can't sleep, I don't sleep.

Tonight, though, had a very different feel. Anna seemed very chilled out and calm. We said our night-nights and then, just before she turned over, with her arms wrapped around her teddy, she looked at the curtains across the room, smiled and waved and said 'night-night' to them. I asked her who she was saying goodnight to, and she said 'the princess in the curtains'. There was no one else in the room at the time. I didn't pay much attention and just tiptoed out, praying that she wouldn't scream for me as she had done recently. My prayers were answered because when I got to the door and took one last peek at her, I could tell by her breathing that she was fast asleep.

For the past six nights Anna has slept soundly and peacefully, and so have I. She tells me that the princess in the curtains watches over her when she sleeps. I don't know

> what to think but what I do know is that Anna isn't scared of being left alone at night any more.

Anna is in absolutely no doubt that she has a princess guardian angel who watches over her. We can all learn from Anna's story, or indeed other stories about children.

All too often when I share stories sent to me about children, adults tell me that they can't be taken seriously because the child is imagining it, but who are we to pass judgement? Study after study has shown that children are more receptive to psychic experiences than adults. In 2009, a university lecturer hit the headlines when he criticised parents for being dismissive when their seven-year-old daughter told them that she saw an angel at her bedside every night, which she felt comforted by. And quite rightly too! Perhaps she had seen an angel. Children, if they are truthful and well, should be taken seriously. They simply enjoy spiritual experiences without questioning whether it is pretend or real.

Children, as Secret of Earth Number Six reminded us, are more likely to see spirit because they have this awesome ability to suspend disbelief. They don't need proof or evidence to believe in something. Sadly, as we get older, and fear and doubt creep in, we gradually lose this ability. Our connection to heaven would deepen, however, if we could reclaim the wonderfully open and unquestioning approach to life that is our birthright.

All too often our grown-up minds make us doubt and question what we feel, see, hear and think, and the more we doubt and question the more difficult it can be to tell if it's our intuition or our insecurities, or just wishful thinking, doing the talking. So what seemed simple and uncomplicated when we were young becomes a minefield of confusion when we grow up. We have no idea if it is heaven or our imagination doing the talking.

Perhaps you've trusted your feelings or your intuition in the past and it has been proved wrong. Perhaps you had a good feeling about someone and then they let you down, or you thought you had a great idea but in time realised it wasn't so great at all. We've all been there.

In retrospect I can see how frequently I ignored or misinterpreted my intuition, and for me nowhere was this truer than in my choice of partners. If I'd listened to my intuition I could have avoided so much pain and heartache because there were always moments early on in each relationship that didn't eventually work out, or ended badly when a clear, calm feeling inside me urged me to back out. But I ignored these feelings because I was scared of being alone. I told myself I couldn't afford to be choosy. I let my fear silence my intuition.

I can recall vividly my very first impression of my first serious boyfriend. The relationship turned ugly when he became abusive but, lacking self-esteem, I stayed with him for far too long. The first time I was introduced to him my hands went icy cold for no reason and I got a twinge of pain in my chest. I looked at his face and it became angular and distorted. I rubbed my eyes and his face went back to normal. At the time, I dismissed all this as nerves but, looking back, I know that it was a divine warning – a warning I ignored to my peril. It was only when I started to listen to the subtle messages my intuition was sending me that my luck in love turned around.

Intuition or imagination?

It is often difficult to know if it's your intuition or your imagination, but over the years I have come to understand that there are key differences between personal thoughts and feelings and divine intuition. I'll list as many as I can think of below in the hope it will help you.

Quiet certainty: When intuition is talking to you through your feelings or thoughts, you just quietly know it or feel it. The feeling of rightness is very different from the noise and chatter of fear, with its long drawn-out and confusing explanations that clatter around in your head. Communications from heaven have a calm clarity about them. The details may change but the central idea or intention will always remain the same. Unlike the voices of fear there won't be twists and turns and confusing changes of direction.

Gentle and uplifting: Guidance from above is also a lot gentler than fear. If the thoughts in your mind or the feelings in your heart are full of self-doubt, anxiety and judgement, they are the voices of fear. Divine guidance is kinder and non-judgemental. If the voices in your head tell you that you are a loser, you always quit, you can't do what it takes, you're stupid, or make you think of worst-case scenarios, then this certainly isn't heaven speaking. It's your fear. Your intuition would never say things to make you feel distressed. Your intuition might tell you that something doesn't feel right, or that something isn't right for you and it's time to move on and try a new direction. There may be no words at all – just a gut feeling that it's time for a change. Divine guidance will be encouraging, energising, positive and empowering. False guidance is the opposite.

Warm and safe: Intuitive wisdom will make you feel safe and warm, like you're being given an invisible hug. The experience will feel natural and somehow familiar. False experiences will, however, feel unnatural and forced and make you feel anxious and cold and afraid. Instead of feeling comforted and watched over, the experience will make you feel all alone in the world.

Lightning bolt: When it's just you doing the thinking, your conscious mind will gradually take control and interpret things for you. However, input from above comes out of nowhere and requires no interpretation because you understand it instantly. It often has nothing to do with what you're thinking about. Divine guidance typically feels like a bolt out of the blue, whilst wrong guidance builds up an argument slowly and gradually in response to your fears.

Leap of faith: Another difference is that our thoughts and feelings are usually ego-based and designed to protect you from failure, disappointment or embarrassment. Heavenly guidance transcends these fears and, although it tends to fit in with your skill set, and is usually related to your interests, it may sometimes require you to make a leap of faith; to try something new or a different approach, or to put your own interests aside to help others. Your thoughts and feelings won't require this of you – their primary motivation is to keep you ego-based – whereas your intuition (the part of heaven within you) knows that the love and good intention within you is limitless.

Motivation: Heavenly guidance always has one motivation, which is to spiritually enrich your life or the lives of others. There will often be no quick-fix solutions and your hard work may also be required. Money and recognition may follow, but these will be added benefits and not the key motivation.

It is my hope that by noticing these key differences your belief in divine guidance, coming to you through your intuition, will grow stronger and stronger. You will just 'know' when it is your intuition speaking, and you will use all your skills and good intentions to create happiness and success for yourself and others. Believing in yourself and your intuitive power will take time, but the stronger your belief, the easier it will be for you to receive guidance through divine thoughts and feelings.

Beyond words

Many people who have had NDEs report heightened intuitive powers following their trip to heaven but, as we are all born with intuitive powers, intuition is a piece of heaven we can all experience on earth. We would be foolish not to notice and nurture it, and let it guide us towards the light. We have all had times when we discovered or knew something without using our five senses. Gradually a whole new world of possibility beyond your senses opens up to you. You can call this intuition, psychic power, inner knowing, sixth sense, gut feeling or the even the real me. I call it heaven.

7. ANGELS

The seventh secret of heaven is an open and glorious secret: **angels**.

My angel up in heaven, I wanted you to know.
I feel you watching over me, everywhere I go.

Anon

Yes, there are angels in heaven. I thought I'd answer that question immediately. Here's Harry's angelic story during a NDE.

Angel in my Pocket

My wife believed in angels but I didn't – I mean, I didn't before my NDE, which occurred two and a half years ago when I was out cycling and got hit by a bus. I lost consciousness immediately. First thing I recall is my head being cradled by the most beautiful angel. It was neither male nor female but I knew it was an angel. I also knew I had nothing to fear and that I was going to be taken care of. The angel had enormous wings, truly enormous. It was like they filled the universe.

The angel lifted me out of my body and I started floating upwards, with the angel carrying me like a wee baby. I could still see my body on the road with passers-by frantically calling for help on their mobiles. It was like I was in two different dimensions – both co-existed with each other. I could see the world below and I also belonged to heaven. Heaven was all around me and I had a sudden understanding that heaven is not a place you go to but a place that co-exists with everyday life. I also saw that hovering beside each person in the road there were one, two or three angels. The people that walked past me without offering to help or giving my situation a second thought in their hearts had angels beside them, but they were small and still beings of light, while those who offered assistance or sent loving, healing thoughts (I could see that too, as emotions in the spirit world are 'alive') had angels beside them that glowed and looked triumphantly, vibrantly happy.

All the time I was with my angel I had this awareness of two worlds: the world where my body lay and paramedics attended, and then my angel world, or heaven. There was so much light in my heaven it was intoxicating. I heard sounds in heaven but not with my ears. I heard with my mind. I could touch, hear, smell, taste and sense heaven, but I had hundreds of other senses too that were not of this world.

The angel told me we were going deeper and we were there. The deeper place was so beautiful. It had a brilliant light all of its own. It looked like a valley but heaven has not allowed me to retain any true memory of it beyond the fact that it was the most beautiful place I had ever seen. Again, while I was there I was also watching myself lying in the road. All the while the angel carried me gently and carefully like a baby. It was the most comforting sensation.

My body was being carried on a stretcher to the ambulance and, at that point, my angel 'asked me' if I believed in angels now. Of course I did, and in that instant I felt a jolt and was back in my body.

I can't prove to you scientifically that heaven is real, all I have is my own personal experience to relate, but I tell you something – I carry a guardian angel everywhere in my pocket now. I'm also acutely aware that there is an angel or two or three on my shoulder. I want to think that what I say, think or do makes them triumphantly happy and proud of me – makes them glow brightly so other spirits will notice me if they pass by.

People typically report meeting an angel in heaven in the form of a brilliant light – a light brighter than any seen on earth. The light doesn't hurt or dazzle them, though. On the contrary, people say that this being of light radiates love and feelings of peace.

Encounters with beings of light are a common aspect of NDE stories but the revelation that we meet angels in heaven isn't really much of a secret, or even a revelation because, since time began, when people have imagined heaven they imagine angels there. In our minds and hearts the two are inseparable.

But what is an angel?

Listed below are the most common descriptions of angels from different cultures. The chances are one or more of them will fit your belief system:

- Celestial beings that act as messengers between heaven and earth
- Spiritual beings or intermediaries that connect God or a higher power with human kind
- A human being who manifests extraordinary goodness, purity and selflessness
- A semi-divine being that comes to earth with a message of goodness and sacrifice for the good of others
- A personification of goodness, light and purity
- Winged messengers of God
- Spiritual beings appointed by a higher power to help, guide and protect us in this life and the next
- Beings of light that exist in a higher spiritual plane
- The invisible presence of truth, goodness, love and light in the world
- The invisible presence of truth, goodness, love and light within a person's heart

Angels are typically described as spiritual 'beings of light' with a vaguely human form, often with wings and a halo. They are said to be beautiful, graceful and awesome to behold because of their divine purity and power. They are often depicted as young women, but NDE accounts report beautiful young men as well or, more commonly, neither male nor female. They are thought to exist in the invisible spirit realm, beyond the boundaries of the natural world as we know it – in other words, heaven.

The word angel (malach) originates from an ordinary Hebrew word meaning 'messenger'. The same is true in Arabic and Greek, and it is the Greek word '*angelos*', also meaning messenger, which is the source for our English word 'angel'. Those coming from a religious background tend to define angels as celestial messengers of God or the divine creator of everything. For others, angels are messengers of love and goodness, but they are not associated with any particular religion. The uniting theme, however, is that they are messengers. In heaven, their role is to escort and guide a spirit to the afterlife and on earth their job is to deliver messages from heaven.

Made of light

Angels are spiritual beings with different bodies to humans, and what they are made of is a matter of debate among different religions and traditions. According to the Talmud, the central text of mainstream Judaism, that dates way back to c 200, the essence of angels is 'fire' that travels upwards towards heaven. Islamic tradition suggests that angels are created from 'light'. From a Christian perspective, the Latin Church father, Saint Augustine of Hippo (AD 354–430) argued that angels were created when God said, 'Let there be light.' The angels are 'light' because they share in the light of God. The word light here means not just light that makes things visible, but the light of wisdom and understanding. Saint Thomas Aquinas (AD 1225–1274) argued in his treatise on angels that they were pure spirits, pure intellect or minds without bodies.

Interesting as this debate may be, it is important to keep in mind that the tradition remains rooted in the concept of angels being, first and foremost, messengers. Saint Augustine declared that the word 'angel' is the description not of their nature, but of their role or purpose. Over the centuries there have been many different interpretations of the angel phenomenon, but the common theme of manifesting or expressing a divine message is always present. Taking this heavenly messenger theme to its logical conclusion, there is no reason why a person, animal, child, feather, cloud or anything else can't be called an angel, if the role taken on is one of a divine messenger of love and joy from the world of sprit.

Every one of us is wonderfully unique in our perception and understanding – our heavenly guides would have us no other way – and therefore there is no correct or incorrect definition of angels. I believe in the individual nature of divine encounters – that celestial beings can take form on earth and in heaven unique to each individual. Each individual's understanding of angels is therefore just as valid as the next person's, because they tend to reveal themselves in the manner that is most comfortable and understandable to you.

If you were to ask me what I believe angels to be, I would tell you that I believe them to be invisible spiritual beings of light from a higher realm that can see the inner light within each one of us. Their task on earth is to help us remember our inner light and the divine potential that exists within each of us. At certain moments in our lives, when our minds and hearts are open, they can connect with our inner light to let us know that we are loved and that this world is not all there is. They look deep into our hearts and see only what is good. They focus only on our inner light. It doesn't matter whether we believe in them or not, because they believe in us and our potential. They want nothing more than to bring love and fulfilment and a sense of purpose into our lives. And their task in heaven is much the same. They are there to guide, comfort and inspire us, as we cross over to the other side and adjust to our new lives in spirit.

Let me stay

Today, belief in angels is steadily on the increase and the ever-increasing flow of NDEs stories involving encounters with angels or beings of light in heaven has to be a contributory factor. These stories confirm that angels are a manifestation of divine love and we will encounter them as beings of light in heaven. Their role or job description, if you can use that kind of terminology, is to assist us as we cross over to the other side, and being in their presence is ecstasy. Typically, when a person has 'met' an angel in heaven, they are unwilling to return to earth. Just remembering the experience fills them with overwhelming feelings of love and compassion.

Tasted Paradise

I didn't want to go back. The angel told me I must go back because there was more for me to do. But I didn't want to go back. That sounds horrible, doesn't it? I love my husband and children and my life on earth so much but when I was in heaven I knew I was home. I was enveloped in love and feelings of bliss. I wanted to stay so I could send some of that love and bliss to my family on earth but the angel told me I needed to do that in my human form. I knew instinctively that I would not feel the same euphoria in my human form, but the angel assured me that when I returned my life would never be the same. The angel was right; my life has not been the same. How can it be? I have tasted paradise. I see the world in a totally different light. I know that death is not the end and that infinite love, joy, beauty and bliss awaits us.

Lily

It isn't just NDE stories, however, that have fuelled belief in angels. Another factor has to be the increasing numbers of people willing to come forward to talk about seeing angels or angel signs on earth – but that's the subject of another book.

Over the centuries many scholars, mystics and writers have felt the need to develop theories about the hierarchy of angels and their 'superiors' – archangels – in heaven. From my close study of NDEs, however, I have found that an angel is an angel; a bright-white light is a bright-white light. There is little talk of rank. This is satisfying for me, as I have often felt uncomfortable with the 'on heaven as it is on earth' theory, where there are angels of higher rank and angels assigned specific roles. I have always believed that angels are simply beautiful manifestations of the divine loving force that sustains everyone and everything in the universe, in this life and the next. They are spiritual beings

– sometimes visible, but more likely invisible, that act as a connection to the divine within us, around us and above us.

Angel or spirit?

NDE accounts shed light on another question I am often asked: are spirits and ghosts of departed loved ones also angels?

The answer is no and yes! A 'spirit' is the soul or spirit of a person who lives on after death. A 'ghost' is also the spirit of a dead person but, unlike a spirit, it is not yet aware it has passed into the afterlife. Both ghosts and spirits can, if witness accounts are to be believed, manifest in human form on earth. Spirits will protect and guide but ghosts will just appear. In contrast to spirits and ghosts, angels have never had a physical presence on earth. They are simply pure beings of love. Sometimes, though, angels will choose to manifest or express their loving energy on earth through the spirits of departed loved ones. In heaven this is not the case, as NDEs typically mention both angels and the spirits of departed loved ones greeting them on arrival.

Both angels and spirits can, it seems, appear on earth in myriad different ways, such as when you hear a voice, see a vision, have a magical dream or coincidence, smell a certain fragrance, witness the appearance of a white feather, and so on, and the messages they bring are always of love and healing. This is why, in my angel books, I often refer to spirits as angels and use the terms interchangeably. I also believe that spirit signs or calling cards, outlined in the next chapter, may also be angel calling cards or signs.

Although my definition of angels and spirits is based on what I have discovered over the years, I have never had a NDE or seen a full-blown angel or spirit on earth, so you may find other definitions or have your own definition. I would have it no other way. The path to heaven is one you must discover for yourself. The point I wish to make is that whenever and however angels are discussed, they are overwhelmingly referenced as benevolent spiritual messengers from heaven. The love angels have for us is unconditional and their role, both on earth and in heaven, is to help us feel and understand the divine energy that is within and all around us, and to which we will return when our time comes to cross over to the other side.

In my opinion, it doesn't really matter what kind of angel or spirit you see or receive or even meet on entry to heaven, just that you are seeing and that what you are receiving touches your heart, because if your heart has been touched you have seen an angel and you have, without being consciously aware, visited heaven.

8. SPIRITS

The eighth secret of heaven is yet another magical open secret: in heaven you are reunited with the **spirits** of departed loved ones.

> *Stars are opening in heaven where our loved ones shine down.*
>
> Anon

Just as most people associate heaven with angels, most people also associate a heaven with a reunion with the spirits of departed loved ones. According to almost every NDE account I have read, there is a reunion with departed loved ones in heaven. These spirits will be familiar to us but, as this intriguing account reported in 2004 by the Dutch cardiologist Pim van Lommel illustrates, some of them not so familiar.

Known but Not Known

During my cardiac arrest I had an extensive experience and I later saw, apart from my deceased grandmother, a man who had looked at me lovingly but whom I did not know. More than ten years later, at my mother's deathbed, she confessed to me that I had been born out of an extramarital relationship. My real father was a Jewish man who had been deported and killed during the Second World War, and my mother showed me his picture. The unknown man that I had seen more than ten years earlier during my NDE turned out to be my biological father.

More typically, though, NDE accounts talk about joyous reunions with those who are very familiar. Shelley wrote and told me that seeing her departed husband in heaven was 'pure bliss' and back on earth she now 'feels him always around her'. Jeremy told me he saw his departed son, who had been disabled in this life, 'laughing and playing football', and Nia said the first people to greet her on the other side were all her grandparents, even one she had never met before, as he had died before she was born. And it's not just departed humans we are reunited with. It seems that beloved pets also greet us. This enchanting message was sent to me by Laura.

First Encounter

You may struggle to accept this – and please don't laugh too much – but I have read many of your books and you often talk about near-death experiences and being met by beings of light and spirits of departed loved ones. Well, after my cardiac arrest, I did feel something all around me, lifting me out of my body. I think they were angels assisting me, and, the higher they lifted me, the more blue and purple colours I saw, felt and heard, yes heard. I think sounds have voices in heaven, everything is alive, everything speaks, including my departed dog, Mary.

This is going to startle you but the first thing I saw clearly as I rose out of my body wasn't family and friends but my little miniature dachshund, Mary. She came bounding up to me and I felt an explosion of joy in my heart. She had died three months previously and I missed her, ached for her so much. She used to go with me everywhere and was so tiny I would put her in my bag when she couldn't walk. She nestled in my lap the way she always used to when she was alive, and then looked at me with her huge, 'love me, feed me, never leave me' eyes.

Then she spoke to me – not 'spoke' as such – it was more telepathy. She told me she would be there waiting for me when it was my time, but it wasn't my time. She told me to take a bit of her back with me. Next thing I remember is waking up with my husband and family gathered around my bed. The first thing I said was, 'Mary. Where is Mary?'

Of course, Mary wasn't there, but in the days, weeks and months that followed she was never far from my mind. I thought about why heaven wanted me to meet her while I left my body and I think I have the answer. Mary taught me the true meaning of unconditional love and that was what I needed to carry back with me to my life – that there is nothing more important in this life and the next than the power of love.

Till we meet again

If you read NDE stories, which are the closest thing we have to proof of heaven, you will see that loved ones, family and friends will most certainly be there waiting for you. Some stories also suggest that it is not just people you have known that greet you, but everyone in the universe because, although we carry our individuality with us into heaven, in spirit everyone is interconnected. This is such a massive concept that our human brain may find it impossible to comprehend, but when I speak to people who have crossed over to the other side and returned to this life, they tell me that in spirit we are all truly one – united by love.

Contrary to popular belief, I believe that the existence of an afterlife, where we are reunited with departed loved ones, is perfectly logical. Just think about it. As explained previously, modern quantum science tells us that everything – you, me, this book, your mobile, keys and so on – consists of energy. Everything in the universe consists of pulsating units of energy, and the manner in which it pulsates determines how it will manifest on earth. Is it so irrational, then, to believe that when our body dies, the energy that sparks us into life – the energy that creates our thoughts and makes our hearts beat – continues to exist? And is it such a stretch of the imagination to think that this energy could live in another realm of existence and continue to interact with the living?

Is it such a stretch to think that our loved ones look down on us from heaven?

If we open our hearts to them, our loved ones can and do look down on us from heaven. Remember, heaven is really a higher state of consciousness and not a place, and even on earth we can live in heaven and feel the presence of departed loved ones. The choice is yours. The place your loved ones went to after death is not up there in the sky. It is around and within you, interpenetrating your life all the time. And those you have loved and lost are not far away, looking *down* on you, they are close by your side on earth, striving to help and guide you, and loving you as they did before they crossed over.

Signs from the afterlife

One way that spirits of departed loved ones try to communicate their heaven-sent love and their constant presence within and around you is through subtle signs or, as I like to call them, divine calling cards. We are so wrapped up in the business of our lives we can fail to notice the signs but, as this story, sent to me by Jordan, shows, heaven sends them all the same.

Where Were You?

When I died and went to heaven everything fell into place. My brother John met me in the tunnel of light. Ever since he died twenty years ago I had missed him greatly, as we were twins and very close, as twins tend to be. He died in a

> motorcycle accident and I had been at a party at the time. He was on his way to pick me up and I felt so guilty. I truly thought because we were so close I would get a sense of him being close to me in spirit but, in all the twenty years since his death, I had felt nothing. When I met him in my NDE he looked so vital and full of joy and love and told me that the guilt I felt about his death was blocking all the love he had been sending me. He told me about the birth of my son and how he was in the euphoria I felt. He told me that he had guided my choice of name (yes, I named my son after John). He told me he had been in every beautiful sunrise and glorious sunset that had taken my breath away. He told me he held my hand as I walked down the aisle to take my wedding vows, and how he tried to take away my sadness that he wasn't there to give me away by blowing a refreshing breeze on my cheeks (as they were hot with tears). He told me about all the moments in my life when I had felt a sense of great joy and how he had been there, inside those moments. He told me he had always been there. I just hadn't noticed him speaking to me.

This story shows that departed loved ones are always sending you signs. When someone you love dies, you long for comfort and often feel totally alone and abandoned, but heaven does respond to your deep longing by sending you signals to reassure and comfort you that you are not alone. Problem is, you often don't notice them, but if you did they would give you extraordinary comfort and hope. All you need to do to receive and notice these signs is open your heart and mind to them.

Calling cards from heaven tend to manifest in unique ways that only the receiver understands, but over the years I have noticed certain signs coming up time and time again. Here's a brief overview:

Visions: I know there are sceptics out there who want absolute proof of life after death. While no one can give absolute proof – although I think near-death experiences come pretty close – visions and images of spirit are pretty awesome. Following is an incredible after-death visit story sent to me by Natasha:

The Visit

Once, when I was fifteen, I was awoken by the feeling of being watched. I glanced up towards the window and my heart stopped as, in front of me, was a slim man whose face looked very familiar. He smiled at me and placed his hand on the windowpane, as though he wanted to come in. I woke up my mother and asked her if she too could see the man standing in the window. She said no and told me to go back to sleep as I was probably dreaming. About ten minutes later I had the same feeling of being watched, I opened my eyes and that same man was kneeling down beside me. He had his arms crossed, was leaning on the bed, and his head was rested on his arms. He was watching me sleep. When I looked at him he smiled down kindly at me and just watched me.

I sat up with a jolt and screamed out loud, waking my mother for the second time that night. I told her what had happened and she said she was taking me to see the doctor. About a month later, my mother and I were looking through some old photographs and I came across a photo of a young man. I recognised him straight away as being the man who had visited me that night. I asked my mother who the man in the picture was, and she said it was my father when he was in his early twenties. She was in disbelief when I told her that he was my mysterious night-time visitor. She said I must have seen the picture before and just remembered it. I knew I had never seen that picture before. I know now that it was my father visiting me to say he was OK and keeping well.

A full-blown vision like this is one of the rarer types of heavenly communication, but such visions can appear to us in solid or translucent form.

Photographs: I have heard many stories of people seeing loved ones or 'orbs' in photos that are taken after a loved one dies.

Invisible touch: Perhaps you have felt a gentle touch or stroke your face, arm, back or hair, but there was no one there. This is a sign your departed loved ones are close by and it can be incredibly comforting – almost as if they are saying, I love you. You may also suddenly sense the presence of a spirit.

Smell: Smell is a very common way for departed loved ones to communicate with us and typically it is something associated with that person in spirit, like a perfume they wore, and you will smell it suddenly, even when the windows or doors are closed.

Dreams: Vivid dreams of departed loved ones are perhaps the subtlest but also one of the first ways the other side may reach out to you. The dream may have felt real and the reason is because it *was* real. Signs that it was a dream visitation mean the departed person is happy and smiling, and it feels like they are still alive. There won't be any words, as communication will be telepathic. You may also wake up feeling emotional.

Objects: This is a common and very effective way for loved ones to get our attention. The object can quite literally be anything, but it will often be something that has significance for you: a special photo or item of jewellery that has been lost and then suddenly found or is moved at significant times. Another common sign is the appearance of a coin in unlikely places or at significant times.

Nature: The natural world is a natural home for heaven to reach out to us. I have been sent thousands of amazing and heart-warming stories about the appearance of unusually shaped clouds, butterflies, flowers, rainbows and other miracles of nature at significant moments. Perhaps the most reported, and the one that touches people's heart's the most, because it has become so associated with angelic visitation over the years, is the sudden and inexplicable appearance of a white feather.

Animals and birds: Spotting animals and birds at unusual times of the year can sometimes feel like comforting signs from the other side to let us know they are at peace.

Numbers: Seeing the same number repeated in phone numbers, car number plates and addresses can be a visual sign from heaven. A lot of people write to tell me that they notice the number 11.11 and when they do it fills them with a sense of awe – anything that fills you with a sense of awe is a sign from above.

Electricals: Lights flickering, clocks stopping and other unexpected experiences that give you pause for thought or make you feel you are being watched can also be signs from the other side.

As with all the signs listed here it is not so much the sign but the timing of them that matters. Typically the sign will appear when a person is in need of guidance or reassurance, perhaps following the death of a loved one or at a crisis point in their life. The perfect timing of the sign is often put down to it being a coincidence but, as we have seen in this book, coincidence or synchronicity is the language that heaven chooses to speak to us on earth.

The miraculous ways our loved ones let us know they are close by never ceases to fill me with wonder. I have no idea how much energy it takes for them to reach out to us, but I'm sure it's a lot, and proves yet again how much they love us. If you don't sense the presence of a departed loved one you may want to relax or do something to put you in a relaxed state of mind, such as walking, meditating or listening to music. It is easier for you to sense their energy when you are in a relaxed, higher vibration state. If you do get a sign – cherish it, trust it and enjoy it. Don't destroy the connection by trying to rationalise it – just be comforted by the certain knowledge your loved ones are never far away, and when your time to cross over comes they will be waiting to greet you with love and joy.

Carrying on

Digressing a bit here, but my heart tells me to linger on the subject of loss a while longer because if you have lost a loved one you will know the deep pain of grief; pain that does eventually ease with time but which you will always carry with you. You are not the same person ever again after loss and nor would you want to be. You carry memories of your loved one with you but I hope Secret Number Eight has shown you that in heaven there will be a reunion. I hope this secret will have also shown you that, although it is deeply painful losing someone close to you, that person lives on inside and all around you.

However strong your belief in heaven, there is no denying that the journey through grief is one of the hardest and most agonising journeys we ever make. After the initial shock, numbness, despair, anger and endless tears subside with time. The sharp intensity of the grief process eases and this is when there is tremendous opportunity for healing. In fact, as mentioned way back in Secret of Earth Number One, the loss of a loved one is often the catalyst for the greatest spiritual growth. Perhaps for the first time in our lives we fully understand that material things can't bring comfort and we then seek spiritual solutions.

Every person grieves in their own way and there is no set formula for healing but I hope these very brief guidelines may help ease the suffering and transform your journey through grief into a spiritually meaningful one.

Never forget: Don't make the mistake I did after my mother died and go into denial or hide every item that triggers memories because that will be a one-way street to even deeper pain further down the line, when it will be impossible to deny the truth of your loss. Instead, celebrate how much that person contributed to your life because of who they were. Feel gratitude and respect for the love they had for you and the home they found in your heart. Remind yourself that although their physical presence has gone away, nothing they gave to you can ever be taken away. They are, and always will be, a part of you.

Forgive: If there was anything you didn't say or wish you had said – or wished you *hadn't* said – forgive yourself, because forgiveness heals your spirit and the spirit of the person you've loved and lost. Holding onto hurt and pain and guilt and fear will clip the wings of your loved one in spirit and your own heart. After my mother died I tortured myself for many years with regret because I wasn't with her when she died. I have since learned that spirits sometimes choose to leave their physical forms unexpectedly, as this makes the transition to their new life on the other side easier for them and for those they leave behind. In other words, they leave in this sudden way by themselves out of love; just as those who linger also stay around on this earth because of love – everything about crossing over to the other side centres around love.

Grow your wings: Recognise that your life changes for ever. The release of the energies that were directed towards your loved one in their physical form can trigger a transformation of your consciousness. Time and time again I have been moved to tears by stories sent to me from people who say that, in time, after a loved one has passed, they experience feelings of great love from an invisible source, like a gift from above. Others grow in self-knowledge and inner wisdom and think more deeply about the meaning of their lives. These peak experiences often trigger a period of further spiritual growth and a deeper, more meaningful life.

Coming together: The passing of a loved one often brings their family and friends together and strengthens bonds of love and support. This is because the life of the person who has departed bonds others together and fosters unity. The bonds formed also honour and celebrate their life. Sometimes, though, due to personal circumstances, you may find yourself alone, coping with your grief without the support of family and friends. If that is the case, comfort and support can be found by turning your mind to meaningful ways to create something lasting to remember them by. Perhaps the creation of a beautiful memorial, or a charity formed in their name, are inspiring examples of something lasting to remember them by and to renew your life.

Cry: I shall keep this simple – don't hold back your tears if you need to cry. Your loved ones in spirit will understand and wrap you in love. It is natural, normal and healthy to grieve for the loss of your physical relationship. Not grieving fully will block the development of your new relationship in spirit. So, if you need to cry, cry and cry some more.

They did not die: This whole book really underlines this point. Although part of the grieving process involves mourning for the loss of a loved one's physical presence, and letting go of physical attachments to them, the death of that person should not be viewed as an ending but the beginning of a new relationship with them in spirit form. In time you will begin to feel their presence and notice the signs of love and comfort they are always sending you. The gentle breeze on your face, the appearance of a significant object, a comforting dream, or any of the signs or heavenly calling cards mentioned above, are a form of communication between your spirits.

I'll close this section with the first few lines of an unspeakably beautiful poem by Mary Elizabeth Frye, 'Do Not Stand at My Grave and Weep', which says what I want to say far better than I ever can. If you are grieving the loss of a loved one, read it daily, several times daily. You will never tire of reading the words, I promise.

Do not stand at my grave and weep.
I am not there; I do not sleep.
I am a thousand winds that blow.
I am the diamond glints on snow.

9. YOU

The ninth Secret of Heaven may come as more of a surprise than the previous two. The ninth secret is **YOU**!

> *If I ever reach heaven I expect to find three wonders there: first, to meet some I had not thought to meet there; second, to miss some I had expected to see there; and third, the greatest wonder of all, to find myself there.*
>
> Confucius

You are divine and here on earth for a purpose. If you want to see heaven, take a good long look at yourself or what is in your heart.

The greatest wonder of all

When we think of heaven we bring to mind the spirits of departed loved ones, angels, clouds, harps and so on, but a vital piece of the puzzle is often missing: our own presence there. I must admit this is often the case for me when I think about the afterlife. I imagine lots of incredible, breathtaking things, but don't picture myself there at all. Perhaps this has to do with lack of self-belief. I know I am a work in progress in that department, as I guess most of us are. Or perhaps it's because only when we cross over to the other side do we fully understand our own divinity.

Let's backtrack to Secret of Heaven Number One: full and complete awareness that you are a spiritual being having a human experience and not the other way round. On earth we catch glimpses of this secret and partially understand it and this transforms our lives into ones lived with profound meaning. But it is only in heaven that we fully comprehend our own divinity. It is only in heaven that we see clearly and without a hint of doubt that on earth we were manifestations of the divine in human form.

As mentioned in previous secrets, sometimes we catch partial glimpses of this life-changing truth on earth with visions, signs, dreams and coincidences. However much we trust and believe and have confidence in the world of spirit, we are still human and there will always be moments of weakness and confusion that we need to work through. In heaven, though, this is not the case. When we pass over we don't lose our individuality but we become one with the divine and have complete awareness of our true spiritual identity. We finally know ourselves. The experience is euphoric.

In heaven we also begin to understand the reason for our lives is to discover who we truly are – in other words, to find out that we are spiritual beings that have chosen to manifest in human form. Our sole purpose is to discover heaven inside ourselves; to rediscover ourselves as spiritual beings.

One way to do this is to start loving ourselves more and recognising that each one of us is a completely and utterly unique miracle. Doing what we love and brings us joy will also take us to a higher spiritual place. You will know when you are living a life of passion and spending your time and energy doing things you love because you'll suddenly lose concept of time, as you'll be lost in the intensity of the present moment. Perhaps the most important path to spiritual awareness, however, is to help others – to dedicate your life to boosting the happiness and wellbeing of others, rather than always thinking how you will benefit personally. If you do the latter you serve your ego and nourish fear. Even if outward success is achieved, you will feel unsatisfied within, but if you do the former you serve your spirit and generate love. Your life will be filled with meaning and purpose and you will naturally attract joy and abundance your way.

The truth is out there

As children we are encouraged to believe in an unseen world, from the tooth fairy to Father Christmas and fairy tales, but as the years pass and reality with its doubts and fears bite, we lose that unquestioning trust in a world greater and more magical than our own. This leaves a big hole in our hearts because, as we have seen during the revelation of the previous eight secrets of heaven, if we lose belief in something it is unlikely to manifest in our lives. If you believe in love and miracles they tend to happen and it's the same with belief in heaven.

NDE accounts teach us that regardless of whether a person believes in heaven or not, it is out there. Not everyone who has a NDE is religious or even spiritual, and a significant proportion had no belief in heaven at all or were atheists before their experience changed everything for ever. Some say the only belief system they had was in themselves, but then their NDE broadened their perspective. Those who were committed to a religion understood that their faith was not essential, merely a starting point for them to experience heaven; those who did not believe in heaven, or thought this life was just about the physical, had their world view shattered beyond recognition.

All NDE accounts teach us that the universe offers each one of us endless possibilities and each one of us has an unlimited potential for spiritual growth and fulfilment. The instant we reach heaven we are infused with an immediate understanding of our spiritual identity and oneness with the divine love that sustains the universe.

As you might expect, NDEs dramatically change people who have had them. Almost without exception each one of them talks about how they now view their lives in a totally different way. They see their lives as deeply meaningful. Some make dramatic changes of career or lifestyle in accordance with this new-found meaning, others quietly continue with their lives but inside they view everything in a different way, focusing their intention and energy on love and kindness and helping others or expressing their unique talents. In other words, living an authentic life of passion.

Some tell me they view their lives as if they are still in heaven and looking down on earth. This helps them strengthen the understanding they have of a strong link between their higher spiritual selves and their human form. They ask themselves daily if their spirits have faith in their human manifestation. Are they loving and compassionate and kind? Are they true to their word? Are they serving others rather than themselves? Are they treating themselves with respect? The more they can answer yes to these questions the more they know they are living a life true to their spirits.

This idea of spiritual accountability and responsibility can extend to each one of us regardless of whether or not we have had a NDE. If you make the choice to believe in love, kindness and respect for others, YOU reveal heaven to others. Living a life of love and kindness also sets off a chain reaction, because simply witnessing kindness inspires the observer to do the same. And when you consider that your actions in this life determine the life you experience in heaven, the stakes are high.

If you believe in love and compassion, that is what will await you on the other side. And if you live a life of love and compassion now, the world becomes a more heavenly place. So by believing in yourself and in the goodness of others, you become the difference that spirit makes in this world. In a nutshell, heaven in this life and the next is all about the amazing YOU.

All about you

I have always been profoundly inspired by the Ghandi quote: 'Be the change you want to see in the world', and the more I have studied and written about heaven the more I think it's the code by which to live our lives and the fast track path to heaven. I think it applies to spirituality, too, in that it could be rewritten to say, 'Be the heaven you want to see in the afterlife'.

Just as it's possible to change the world around us by improving our own lives, it is possible to create an afterlife sparkling with love, beauty and magic starting with our thoughts, words and actions. In this life we all have our own unique struggles to live and grow through, but inside each one of us there is a beautiful spiritual light that can bring hope into the darkness. We see this light shining most brightly when we are babies and people rejoice in our beauty and light. Then time takes its toll and people start making us question and doubt ourselves. Over time we don't need other people to question and doubt us because we have learned to do it to ourselves. Sometimes this doubt is so strong you can't see or even remember the light any more but then, out of nowhere, memories flood back. Perhaps the trigger was the kindness of another person or the beauty of nature or reading a NDE or an unexpected moment of joy and inspiration or this book? Whatever the trigger, we suddenly sense we are more interconnected than we will ever know and this loving glow from within inspires us to see our own beauty. We start to glow brighter in our daily lives. We feel better, happier and more alive and, as we stop doubting ourselves, we also stop doubting others, and they shine brighter as a result of our belief in them.

The most important path to a more meaningful life is trusting and loving yourself. Glimpsing our own beauty and divinity is a sensational feeling, a divine feeling that gives you strength and, although slumps back into the darkness are inevitable, as to be human is to be fragile, the process of spiritual development has begun and your life is never, ever the same again. You begin to surprise and astonish everyone around you with your own beauty, but the person you surprise the most is yourself.

Secret of Heaven Number Nine reminds you that you have a spiritual light – a piece of heaven – inside you that is magical and beautiful and can guide and comfort you on earth and take you by the hand when your time comes to step into heaven. This light wants you to love who you are, to be true and honest in all your dealings with others, to treasure those you love and, most importantly of all, to let yourself be happy.

Be happy

The kind of happiness I'm talking about here is not smiling from the mouth but from the heart. It is the otherworldly joy that brings tears of bliss to your eyes when you hug someone you love, or take in a wonderful view or listen to beautiful music. It is the kind of joy that fills you with feelings of love, compassion and awe and, once you experience it, you will know that evolving spiritually is the only thing that really matters in your life and gives your life true meaning.

And while we are on the subject of the meaning of life, perhaps more than anything Secret of Heaven Number Nine reminds you that you are here on this earth for a reason. You have an important purpose and destiny and that is to grow spiritually and find heaven from the inside out. Once you discover who you really are you become an inspiration to others, revealing your inner light, and, through everything you say and do, the presence of heaven on earth.

So, although there are many astonishing secrets of heaven revealed by NDEs it is important not to forget – as we all tend to do – that perhaps the fastest, simplest and most honest, purest and most powerful way is to just look in the mirror.

10. LOVE

The tenth, and most powerful secret of all, because it encompasses and overshadows all the other Secrets of Earth and Heaven, is **love**.

> *Of all the music that reached farthest into heaven, it is the beating of a loving heart.*
>
> Henry Ward Beecher

As I sat down to begin this last section, news from Paris about the shooting of innocent people in a restaurant, theatre and football stadium by religious militants (now there is an oxymoron if ever there was one) hit the headlines. It brought me right back to 2001, when I was working on my psychic encyclopaedias and witnessed the tragic events of the twin towers unfold on the TV screen with depressing and terrifying finality. My heart and thoughts went immediately to the final moments of the victims. What fear and terror and what pain! But then, in the days ahead, just as it was with victims of 9/11, and also 7/7 in London and other atrocities, eye-witness accounts and reports from Paris focused on one message only – love.

The final words the victims uttered or heard were typically not of hate but simple 'I love you' messages to family and friends. And in the same way, although the relatives of the victims made public their contempt for the atrocities, they also made it clear that they would not give the deluded individuals who perpetrated the attacks the gift of their hate. One particularly poignant message came from the father of a young child, visiting the scene of the bombings in Paris to lay flowers. The little boy asked his father how they could fight back and the father replied, 'We fight them with flowers.' If ever words were heaven-sent, those were.

> *Darkness cannot drive out darkness; only light can do that. Hate cannot drive out hate; only love can do that.*
>
> Martin Luther King

Love on the other side

If you ask most people what they think love is they'll probably talk about romantic love or the unconditional love a parent has for a child, or the platonic love families and friends have for each other, or the intellectual's love for art and beauty. However, NDE accounts show that although these kinds of love are certainly aspects of love they are not the whole; love is far greater than passion or familial bonds. People who have died and gone to heaven talk about love as the most powerful energy in the universe. Love in heaven is much more intense than that of earthly romance – it is divine energy of such blinding force it completely engulfs us. It is so powerful and all-consuming and profound, that it's impossible to fully understand or express in words. I think Sara's story below has something very insightful to add here about the nature of love in heaven:

The Power of Love

Now that I have gone public about my NDE, people constantly ask me how it felt and what I saw. I try to be specific but it's hard because no words can really describe it but perhaps this anecdote will help. When I was in the tunnel the light asked me if I wanted to stay and I said I did. The light then told me I couldn't and I asked why I couldn't. I told the light that I tried on earth to be a decent human being, to love and take care of others. The light then asked me if I had ever loved anyone else the way I had been loved here and I said that of course I hadn't because I was human. The light beamed brighter and told me I had to go back to prove myself wrong, as I could love so much better.

Those who have been to the other side have glimpsed the true, earth-shattering power of love and they also know that who or what we love on earth is a reflection of who we are or need to become in order to grow spiritually. We give and seek love in our lives because we are seeking to connect with the divine, to become spiritually whole. Seen in this light, there is nothing more powerful and important than love. It is the reason for our being.

Take yourself lightly

Possibly the only thing that comes close to love as a force is joy and laughter. I'm not talking about comedy put-downs, but the genuine good-natured joy that unites people intimately. One of my major problems with religion and also even spiritual groups and retreats (and I've joined and been on many of those in my life) is the total absence of laughter. It is all so deadly serious.

The new age movement is as guilty as any other spiritual group when it comes to the absence of humour. I recently went to a talk about spiritual growth and development and the person leading the group was even involved in running laughter workshops, but the whole meeting was totally devoid of good humour. This is not uncommon and it's one of the major reasons I've long since stopped attending retreats, workshops and seminars. Learning about heaven is becoming too deadly serious for my taste. I have always loved this G.K. Chesterton quote:

Angels can fly because they take themselves lightly.

This isn't to say you should be inappropriate in your humour but to point out that when you laugh you open your heart to divine love; you let love in. When you laugh with someone else you create harmony and help them connect with the divine love already within them.

Life should be as enjoyable as possible. Many of us are unhappy because we base our happiness on things we think we need to acquire or achieve, but NDE accounts show that none of these things ultimately matter. Heaven is not interested in your bank balance, your waistline, or how many likes you have on Facebook. Heaven is only interested in your heart, your essence, and your capacity to love, but you can't be a loving person unless you are happy yourself.

And what is the secret of being a happy person? Simple. First it is to love yourself. You can't be happy if you don't like yourself. And what is the secret to liking yourself? Simple. It is doing meaningful work and being of service to others.

When you approach life with love and good humour and the belief that you are a good person, the world begins to reflect that back to you. If there are disappointments along the way you become wiser, stronger and more loving as a result. Whatever your goals in life, and however you chose to express your unique talents, love remains the only certain path to heaven. In short, dedicating yourself to love and the loving service of others ensures that your life becomes a representation of heaven on earth.

Heaven is not for the faint-hearted

The more of us that recognise and connect with the love inside us, the more we bring peace and harmony to the world. Love is an abundant and limitless energy and the more we give it freely and without expectation of return, the more love is created. In this way our loving thoughts and deeds transform the world one heart at a time, from one of conflict into one of love.

Loving and helping others with no expectation of return is a big and sometimes impossible ask. Being human there will be times when we simply can't be selfless because we feel someone or something has taken so much from us that we 'deserve' a return. But to take you back to earlier in this section, and the little boy being told by his father to fight hate with flowers, the only way to bring heaven to earth is to aspire to this kind of spiritual love. You need a huge amount of courage to love in this way. Love is not for the faint-hearted.

Love is not an option for the feeble. Those who have seen heaven testify to the indescribable might and power of love and how it pulsates through all that is, including each and every one of us, and how the only way for us to grow in power is to not withhold love and jealously guard it for ourselves, but to give it freely to others.

Many people tell me, especially in the wake of disasters and tragedies, that they feel ineffective and they can't see the point in trying to be the change they want to see, as they are just a tiny dot on a huge planet. I tell them this could not be further than the truth. I reference NDE accounts that show that, on the other side, love is who we are and who everyone is. Love unites us all. We are all one. I tell them there is more power in one single loving heart than in a thousand armies. You are making a difference if you chose to dedicate your life to love and to extending yourself in kindness towards others. You may not always see the impact your loving heart is making on the universe, but in heaven every beat is heard loud and clear and strengthens the forces of light against the forces of darkness.

You see, when you love yourself and others this is when you are most connected to heaven. If you are looking for a magic cure to all that is wrong in the world or that troubles you, you can find it within your own heart. If you are looking for proof of heaven all you have to do is truly love.

Love survives death

We can learn so much about heaven from NDE accounts but, to risk repeating myself, there is always one overriding and ever constant theme: love is the essence of our lives here on earth, and love is what we take with us and what we meet and become one with on the other side. I could not think of a better way to conclude this section than with the following. Take your time reading these, as I truly believe they hold a concise summary of the secrets of eternal life.

> *In short, near-death experiences present us with a universal, all-inclusive, perfectly integrated spiritual path that revolves around three core truths: 1. We are all one; 2. Love is the essence of life; 3. We are here, in this world, to become perfect embodiments of the divine.*
>
> David Sunfellow

> *I have never interviewed anyone who had a near-death experience who told me that they came back to make more money or to spend more time at their jobs away from their families . . . Instead, they become convinced that they need to be more loving and kind. They react to their experience by living life to its fullest. They seem*

to know that the love they create while living will be reflected and radiated back to them when they die.

Melvin Morse

Magic exists. Who can doubt it, when there are rainbows and wildflowers, the music of the wind and the silence of the stars? Anyone who has loved has been touched by magic. It is such a simple and such an extraordinary part of the lives we live.

Nora Roberts

Final Word: Seeing Your Light

And now I will show you the most excellent way. If I speak in the tongues of men and of angels, but have not love, I am only a resounding gong or a clanging cymbal. If I have the gift of prophecy and can fathom all mysteries and all knowledge, and if I have a faith that can move mountains, but have not love, I am nothing. If I give all I possess to the poor and surrender my body to the flames, but have not love, I gain nothing.

Love is patient, love is kind and is not jealous; love does not brag and is not arrogant, does not act unbecomingly; it does not seek its own, is not provoked, does not take into account a wrong suffered, does not rejoice in unrighteousness, but rejoices with the truth; bears all things, believes all things, hopes all things, endures all things.

Love never fails . . . But now faith, hope, love, abide these three; but the greatest of these is love.

1 Corinthians 13:4-7,13

The Secrets of Heaven revealed by NDE accounts can open your eyes, minds and hearts to the possibility of heaven within and all around you in this life and the next. They show that there is so much more to this life than we are capable of understanding in our human form. The more I read about and research NDEs, the more I begin to understand what heaven is truly like or sense things about the meaning of this life that I never did before.

Perhaps the best analogy I can think of is if you spent your entire life living in a cave, thinking the cave is all there is, then you suddenly stepped outside into the light, this would be an overwhelming experience. You would suddenly realise there is a whole world that you never knew existed. Then, if you are asked to go back and live in the cave again after what you have seen, you will never be the same again because you'll have seen what clarity and light exists outside. You can never forget the outside word. It becomes your reference point and, because of your experience of the bigger picture outside your current existence, you understand and approach things in a totally different way.

Although this book can't actually take you to heaven I truly hope it has helped you escape from your cave and see your light outside. I also hope it has given you a glimpse of heaven and life on the other side.

The end of the tunnel

As this entire book has been informed and inspired by NDE accounts, I feel my closing comments should pay tribute to the remarkable and truly visionary work of two doctors: Raymond Moody and Sam Parnia.

Psychiatrist Raymond Moody, M.D. devoted his career to interviewing thousands of people who had died and come back to life and he wrote the first bestselling books about the subject.

What is most stunning about the groundbreaking research he did was the remarkable consistencies and similarities between the stories he uncovered. Each person was drawn towards a tunnel where they could see a bright light at the end, into which they stepped and were greeted by a flood of unconditional love which they recognised as their essence and the force that sustained the universe. Each person felt an overwhelming sense of peace and joy that they had never experienced on earth. They could also see the impact of all their earthly actions on others and witnessed a panoramic view of their entire life. Moody really did the groundwork for all future researchers and writers about this incredible phenomenon by bringing the subject into the spotlight as never before in his 1975 book, *Life After Life*, in which he coined the term near-death experience. As a result, he is now recognised as the father of NDE psychology.

Fast-forwarding to the present day, Doctor Sam Parnia is pushing the boundaries even further with his own groundbreaking research involving thousands of patients all over the world who have experienced NDEs. The conclusions he has tentatively drawn from interviewing patients who have 'died', appear to actually prove the survival of consciousness after death. His research is so convincing that even sceptics are paying attention. Exciting times lies ahead, as he plans an even larger study.

Without the tireless work of these two men (and, of course, improvements in resuscitation techniques that enable people to return to life where they would have previously died), it is unlikely we would have so much knowledge about what happens when we die. Death used to be the greatest secret of all but now the veil has well and truly begun to lift.

There are many scientists who disagree with Moody, Parnia and other NDE researchers. Many convincing theories have been put forward to explain the near-death experience, of which the most prevalent is that the brain is hallucinating or shutting down or is influenced by strong drugs often administered at the end of life. Both Moody and Parnia have been able to offer evidence to refute this argument by referencing patients who have witnessed things it was impossible for them to witness, or where they have uncovered information they did not know before.

As compelling as the scientific search for full-blown proof of heaven is, perhaps the most surprising thing NDE research has uncovered is that the big events of our lives, and the things on which we place a high value, such as money, appearance, status and success, are rarely centre stage during the life review. Instead, it is the simple acts of love and kindness that receive the spotlight. Time and time again, people say they are told to come back to earth because they have more to give others, even though most say their preference would have been to stay in heaven. They have seen the light at the end of the tunnel and want to stay there.

This is small comfort for people who have lost loved ones, but perhaps the reason they stay in heaven is that, however short their life-span, they have fulfilled their destiny in regards to the impact they have on the hearts and minds of others. They have made their mark, and their function now, in heaven, is to inspire those of us left behind to grow in love and spirit.

The final word . . . belongs to your heart

If I was asked to sum up what I had learned from years of studying thousands of afterlife accounts it would be, 'Everything is about love'. We come to earth to learn how to love unconditionally, and when we go to heaven we step into a world of unconditional love.

Love is the secret of life and the secret of death and love is what gives our lives joy and meaning. It can sometimes be hard to understand that love really is the key to eternal life, especially if you have suffered, but the only true and lasting way out of the darkness is love without the expectation of anything in return.

There is no guarantee that others will love you as you would want to be loved, because love is always a choice, but I can guarantee that the love you choose to give freely will always return to live inside your heart. For, in the love you give to yourself and others, lies the seed of heaven. Love has the power to transform the hell of any suffering into heaven.

In the days, weeks, months and years ahead, if you start doubting that heaven is real don't trust your head – there is often too much fear and doubt there – trust your heart, and have the courage to dream, for what you dream can become your life. If you are scared to dream for fear of disappointment, remember the path to heaven begins in your dreams. If you're scared of opening your heart because you fear it might be broken or disappointed, remember it's always better to have your heart broken than to try to escape heartache. A broken heart can be reborn, but a heart engaged in battle cannot die or live, nor know the wonder and beauty of love at all.

Learn to listen to your heart. It's your connection to spirit, to other people, to the universe, and to yourself. The journey of a thousand miles begins with one step. The journey to heaven and eternal life always begins within your heart.

In essence, your heart is on your left, but it is always right.

The Ten Secrets of Earth and Heaven

The Ten Secrets of Earth

1. Awakening
2. Inspiration
3. Courage
4. Confidence
5. Attraction
6. Inspiration
7. Kindness
8. Gratitude
9. Revelation
10. Death

The Ten Secrets of Heaven

1. Awareness
2. Prayer
3. Choice
4. Possibility
5. Calm
6. Intuition
7. Angels
8. Spirits
9. You
10. Love

Calling All Light Seekers

Last, but by no means least, if at any point when reading this book you felt confused or have a story or insight you would like to share with a wider audience in my future books, or have a burning question you need answered or want to discuss further, please don't hesitate to get in touch with me.

You can contact me via my website www.theresacheung.com and my email angeltalk710@aol.com. I would be honoured to hear from you and will answer every question or discuss any issue personally. Sometimes things get really busy letter and email wise so it may take a month or two before I reply but I will reply as soon as I can. Alternatively, for a more immediate response, you may want to meet fellow truth seekers via my Facebook Theresa Cheung Author site. And if you prefer writing letters you can write to me c/o Simon & Schuster, 1st Floor, 222 Gray's Inn Road, London, WC1X 8HB.

Please don't feel alone in your quest for the light. I truly welcome all your thoughts, questions and stories. Communicating with you is the thing I love most about writing books that explore the reality of heaven.

Eternal words

To love is to receive a glimpse of heaven.

Karen Sunde

Only one book is worth reading – the heart.

Ajahn Chah